Dr Perry Crofts studied medicine at the University of Warwick before moving to South Wales to work as a doctor. He enjoys heavy metal and cats.

To my mother, for being a role model.
To my brothers, for being there for me.
To Sophie, for being my rock.

And to everybody going through what I did. For being brave enough to keep going. If I can do this, you can, too.

Dr Perry Crofts

THE COST OF CARING

AUSTIN MACAULEY PUBLISHERS™
LONDON • CAMBRIDGE • NEW YORK • SHARJAH

Copyright © Dr Perry Crofts 2022

The right of Dr Perry Crofts to be identified as author of this work has been asserted by the author in accordance with section 77 and 78 of the Copyright, Designs and Patents Act 1988.

All rights reserved. No part of this publication may be reproduced, stored in a retrieval system, or transmitted in any form or by any means, electronic, mechanical, photocopying, recording, or otherwise, without the prior permission of the publishers.

Any person who commits any unauthorised act in relation to this publication may be liable to criminal prosecution and civil claims for damages.

All of the events in this memoir are true to the best of author's memory. The views expressed in this memoir are solely those of the author.

A CIP catalogue record for this title is available from the British Library.

ISBN 9781528992503 (Paperback)
ISBN 9781528992510 (ePub e-book)

www.austinmacauley.com

First Published 2022
Austin Macauley Publishers Ltd®
1 Canada Square
Canary Wharf
London
E14 5AA

Chapter One
Spitting Blood

There was blood in my sink.

I scrubbed my teeth again and spat into the running water. More blood.

Good, I thought, *Hopefully I have leukaemia.*

Self-loathing ran over me.

My grandmother had died of leukaemia when I was young. I recalled my mother sitting in an armchair in my childhood home, looking lost and sad one day when I had gotten home from school.

I recalled my father sitting my brother and I on my bed to tell me my grandmother had died last night.

The self-loathing was justified.

I deserved leukaemia for daring to hope that I would have it: *I'm a horrible, ungrateful, nasty, little man! I want to die just because I'm too weak and stupid to appreciate my comfortable little life.*

I gripped the basin and opened my mouth in a silent scream, shuddering with the effort.

My housemate was in the next room and I didn't want him to hear anything.

I chastised myself again, *Don't make any noise. I don't want him knowing I'm pathetic too, Do I?* I tapped my toothbrush on the edge of the sink. The noise was an assault, loud and sharp. But it dragged me away from my spiteful internal monologue and into the room.

I kept on tapping, that high pitched note reverberating off the tiled walls of the bathroom and put the toothbrush back gently into its pot.

I looked up from the sink at the reflection in the mirror. A double chinned, curly haired sad sack of a man stood there.

I hated that man in the mirror.

If I had the energy, I would have let that show on my face.

But, instead, two lifeless eyes above dark rings existed back at me. They didn't stare, they didn't scrutinise or observe, they just existed. I thought about how he was a drain on the world, how all of the privilege he had done nothing to deserve was wasted on him, how he was a fat, unlovable blight on everyone who had ever known or cared about him. His hobbies and interests were stupid and a waste of time. He was an unskilled, incapable selfish excuse for a man. About how, if he wasn't such a coward, he would kill himself and do everybody a favour.

I turned away, thinking how the thing in the mirror was winning: his entitlement to exist filling me with genuine rage.

I walked over to my bed where I would spend the next eight hours lying awake, torturing myself with my mind, wishing for sleep or death. One of the two.

I chastised myself that my room wasn't tidy enough, that I didn't change my bed sheets often enough, that I didn't have matching pyjamas.

I'm disgusting, I'm going to sleep in that filth pit I call a bed, in this room I've let get into like the state of a child.

I lay in bed, turned off the lights and spent from nine pm to five am planning my suicide.

I thought about renting a boat and tying cinder blocks to my feet with heavy chains and jumping over-board so that nobody would have to find the body.

I thought about a cliff in the Gower on a sunny, windy day where I could stare out at the sea as I shot myself.

I thought about setting myself on fire, hanging, knives, thick plastic bags and razor blades.

Even I thought about stealing drugs from the hospital to take my own life with.

But then I thought about my mother and brothers. They'd be devastated, wouldn't they? I can't do that to them. I can't actually be that selfish.

After eight hours of pleading with myself for sleep, wretched and desperate, I got out of bed and went to the gym. Everyone in there was stronger, fitter, thinner, funnier, smarter, drove a nicer car and had a better job.

They were all laughing at me floundering on the chin up bar, out of breath at something they would have been able to do while having a chat. In the changing rooms they whispered amongst themselves about the order I kept my toiletries or the colour of shirt I chose to wear.

Everything I did was inferior to everything everyone else did, because fundamentally I was. I kept my head down and gaze averted so nobody would look at or speak to me.

I drove to work in my big posh car, which was supposed to make me happy, while listening to songs meant to do the same. On the motorway I keep my foot pressed down on the accelerator, pressing my foot as hard onto the floor as I could, feeling the surge of power a few seconds after as the turbo kicks in.

"A bloody turbo? Who do I think I am?"

I'm going at over one hundred miles per hour in the fast lane. I take my hands off the wheel, reach down and unbuckle my seatbelt, close my eyes and slowly count to ten.

The only thought that forced me to open my eyes was that if I did succeed in crashing and killing myself, I might cause somebody else to do the same.

They didn't deserve that.

Only I did. When I open my eyes, I'm still in the middle of the lane, I'm going over one hundred now. I take my foot off of the accelerator, indicate, come off the motorway and go to work.

I switched off my car and rested my head on the steering wheel. Lightly enough, not to have the momentary silence shattered by the horn. I gripped the leather of the wheel between my hands so tight my knuckles went white. Twisting it, trying to tear it apart. My mind, ablaze, shrieked at me, not with words or sentiment, just a mental scream in response to the continuous pressure and pain my mind was in.

I breathed in deeply through my nose, summoning my last reserves of optimism. It was as if the rational part of me was pleading with my illness to just let me have today.

"Just stay positive today. Nothing is actually wrong with me! I'm healthy and have everything anybody could ever want. I'm just not trying hard enough to be happy. So pull yourself together, man up, get over yourself and stop being so miserable."

I promised myself I'd be pleasant and optimistic. As I walked in to work a group of nurses walked past me.

"Morning, Per! Been on nights, have we?"

"No, I just look like this," I came back with a reply quickly, a big false smile on my face.

Everybody laughed.

That day I remember being jealous of the cancer patients. They had a way out. They had a reason to feel like this. I longed for an illness or a diagnosis to vindicate my melancholy.

On call that day, every request was met with nothing but venom from me. Every referral or task was an unreasonable request from somebody I despised. In turn, I was greeted with exasperation by the staff on every ward I went on. It was vicious a circle. I hated myself for being alive and taking it out on them. My colleagues disliked me because I was so unpleasant to be around. Everybody was so obviously tired of me. Their short replies and obvious dislike fed the indiscriminate disdain I held for everybody… and most of this was aimed at me.

Day after day, interaction after interaction this point was hammered home: "I hate everybody and everybody hates me. And that's because I'm a petty, broken little man."

When it came to seeing patients, I would beam a big smile, make a joke, take their blood, feel their abdomen and listen to their stories.

We would all smile and laugh, order investigations and begin treatment. I eased pain, diagnosed conditions, every now and then I would save a life. Patients were my reason to stay alive and my escape. I could be completely absorbed in their stories and their care. For a brief few minutes that nasty little voice in my head would be silenced.

I was convinced my work was the only thing which justified my pitiful existence: as long as I was a doctor I mattered. That was the only thing I brought to the world.

"Just imagine… if you weren't good at taking exams? You were lucky to be born smart, that's the only reason you can even approach having any worth. And it's luck! You're not kind or caring. You're lucky and too stupid to realise it!"

I would make dirty jokes to colleagues and have them all laughing: "Oh what's he like?"

"Oh, you can't say that."

I would talk about girls I was seeing, nights out with friends. Nobody had a clue. I would often be on autopilot, engaged in conversations while I screamed from behind my eyes at myself for being such a fraud.

I drove home from work with no sense of relief that it was over. All I had waiting for me at home was hours of fatigue and that same hellish internal monologue.

If my house mate was in, we would talk. It would be exhausting for me and I felt bad because he was a good person and he deserved my attention. But having to maintain some visage of normality for one second longer than I had to wasn't something I often had the energy for.

I shuffled into my, once spotless, kitchen. Crockery was piled on the messy work tops. I didn't have the energy to clean it now.

"Lazy pig. Disgusting." I knew I needed to eat. But I'd lost any interest in food.

"It's for the best, you know, you're a walking time bomb of diabetes. Then you'll be costing everybody else money just because you can't control yourself."

I decided I wasn't going to eat. Other nights I would try and overcome my lack of interest with the sheer quantity of food. Often greasy, fried, junk food. I hated myself the whole time I was ordering it. Even more as I gorged myself on it… but was unable to stop. One of the greatest pleasures in life was now being used by my own mind to torture me.

I walked into the living room and picked up my guitar. Nothing in life brought me as much joy as music but my fingers moved sluggishly over the strings. My ears didn't register what I was playing. It was hollow. Nothing brought me any joy any more: books, games, music, socialising.

It was all there. But it was all meaningless and empty. I tried so hard to devote more time and effort to them. Too tired to crawl out from under this heavy, heavy cloud. To escape the running commentary I provided myself with. But nothing meant anything anymore.

Just to feel anything, other than this numbness so heavy it hurt, would have created a pin-prick of light at the end of this dark tunnel. It would have given me some hope. And hope was in short supply.

My night time routine repeated itself.

Hours of planning my suicide, punctuated by scrolling through social media. Comparing the misery of my existence to the highlights of everybody else's.

"Why could they have this, and I couldn't?" I had to be fundamentally flawed, lacking in some crucial way that made me unworthy of this smiling, 'Group photo life' experienced by my friends.

Between this, I would occasionally snatch an hour of broken sleep – which was never accompanied by either dreams or nightmares. On nights before a day off I would self-medicate: taking handfuls of over the counter sleeping pills or others I had ordered over the internet. I would spend the next day in a sedated fugue which only served to further the gulf between me and everybody else.

And this was my life. For eighteen months this was my life.

A constant monologue, bitter, cruel and nasty. A lack of interest in anything... a complete absence of anything resembling happiness.

No sleep. No appetite and an exhaustion I can't put in to words. It hadn't always been this way and it happened so slowly and subtly that I didn't even notice it. I think it would be hyperbolic to say I lost everything.

I still had friends, I still went out, had a fulfilling job as a doctor. Everything was still there. It just didn't matter.

I was acting a part. I was the happy eccentric doctor. But beneath the act, was pain. A physical pain caused by my own mind, and a hatred of myself with an intensity I've never been able to apply to any other feeling.

I had wanted to die so much. To put an end to my suffering and kill the person I hated, the person whose mind was causing me all that pain in one decisive action.

I no longer think like that.

It was a difficult and painful process to get here and I have to work on it every day. I've made mistakes and struggled along the way.

I have realised I had an illness, gotten help and learned to manage it. Now I enjoy my life and can cope with the bad days.

This book is written for myself, as catharsis, but hopefully for other people as a source of hope.

You can get better.

You are not alone.

This is not permanent.

Chapter Two
No Reason

I have suffered from bouts of depression without realising what it was for my whole life.

It was there, quite unpleasant, but never acknowledged. I never saw it for what it was. Just viewing it as the way things were, or me being a bit dramatic. I think depression runs in the family. I had heard people mention suicide but no specifics, a relative I was close to when I was younger recently committed suicide. That hit me hard. It hit everybody hard.

At their funeral, I remember looking at the coffin. There was sadness there for sure, but, as disgusted as I am in myself for writing this, there was some jealousy there, too. They had found the way out and unlike me, had (what I thought at the time) the determination to follow through with it.

I understood why they had done what they did. I was so ill myself. So locked in to that way of thinking that I saw suicide as something some people just had to do. Something I might one day have to do.

But now that I'm recovering, I see it for what it is: a tragedy. A mistaken belief that it is the only option, to put an end to the hell their lives have become. I wish they could have had time to make the realisations I have. I wish so many people could.

I stood in the back of the church, next to my two brothers but so distant from them. All I could think about was that my relative was at peace now. They had escaped the pain and hopelessness.

I wondered what people would be saying at my funeral when I killed myself. Not if, but when.

That awful voice in my head whispered spitefully in my ear: "How can I be thinking of myself at a time like this? That should be me in that coffin. Not them."

Slowly, I scanned the church. Looking at the faces of the family members that my relative had left behind… of the people in the church, with tears streaming down their cheeks, grief contorting their faces, and posture.

Even more distressing were the faces without expression, incapable of showing the depth of their sadness. The weight of their loss rendering their faces inert.

Except the eyes. Those eyes, large and pleading, they will stay with me. The way they looked around for something to cling on to, maybe hoping to see the person in the coffin stood there with them. The way their voices were quiet and flat. No human quality to them. Nothing more than structured breath.

And yet, looking at all of this suffering, people I'd spent Christmas and birthdays with, completely broken. The thought that people would feel that way about me when I did it never entered my mind.

I was just scalding myself internally: "How can I make this about me? About my imaginary funeral?"

I knew nobody would mourn for me. I imagined a weight lifted from my family's shoulders. No mask-like faces at mine. Just a few silent people attending, out of obligation.

I made a mental note to find out how to donate my body to science. I'd probably be more use as meat. I'd already put some money away to pay for my funeral so that it wouldn't be a stress for my mother.

Now that I'm recovering, I see that it was pain and desperation that led my relative and so many others to taking their own life. The fact that I was jealous of them was just a symptom of my own illness. I'm shocked at how I didn't even notice that my thinking was so distorted. It seemed like the only sensible thought at the time. I hated myself for being so selfish.

But I think suicide is rarely selfish. Until you have been in the position where taking your own life genuinely does seem like the better option than any alternative.

When the people you love being left to pick up the pieces, isn't enough to stop you doing it? I don't think you can comment.

Take a minute to think of the person you love more than anybody else in the world.

Think of the most precious memory you have with that person. That first kiss. The first time you held them after they were born. An indescribable, perfect moment on an otherwise unremarkable, overcast day on the sofa.

When you watched them, without them knowing, and them simply existing filled you with a warmth and a joy that you couldn't name or describe.

So instead of telling them you loved them or holding their hand you just savoured that moment. How that warm, joyful feeling spread out from the centre of your chest and you couldn't help but notice it.

Really think about that most perfect moment and hold it in your mind's eye. Think about how you would do anything to make that person's life better and how much they mean to you.

Now imagine if that person you were thinking of killed themselves. How would you feel? Really think about it.

The loss, the anger, the helplessness. The overwhelming grief, taking you to your bed: weeping, not eating, drinking too much, the time off work. All of it.

When I was beginning to entertain suicide, I knew that was how my family would feel. I even did this exercise in my head to try and stop myself wanting to take my own life.

But eventually it wasn't enough. That it was permanent, and they may never recover, went from being a deterrent to an inescapable consequence to just something that didn't even enter my head.

Imagine that, understanding how much people would suffer, wasn't enough to stop you. Eventually I genuinely believed they would thank me for doing it. That it would make their life better.

Now, don't tell me suicide is, "Just selfish."

It's a consequence of an illness. The same as coughing is a consequence of pneumonia or shitting yourself is a consequence of the norovirus.

I've always been sensitive and prone to sadness. When I was a child, I was cripplingly lacking in confidence, overweight and short.

I hated everything about myself even from primary school. I would have teary-bouts which would concern my mother. I was pre occupied with death and gore and the idea of myself dying. One memory I have is being in the final year of primary school, stood at the top of the stairs hearing my parents whisper about my lack of confidence and tearyness.

I went to an all-boys secondary school and suffered from bullying for a few months, with one particularly nasty incident involving me being tied to a fence, blindfolded and beaten with sticks.

You have to spend the next five years with these people so you had better learn to get on with it.

I didn't avoid school or stop eating. I was actually quite resilient about the whole thing. Luckily, the bullying stopped. I got on quite well with most people and was well liked. I found a niche with the other boys who liked skateboarding. Played guitar in bands with my friends and went out all weekend. I was happy. But despite all of this, I always believed I was different to other people.

Worth less than them. As if they were in a club, they didn't want me to know about, let alone be a part of.

I was a high achiever, often invited to socialise but I liked to be alone.

Friends would sometimes come to my door asking if I would come out and I would ask my mother to lie to them. Saying I wasn't in. I just couldn't handle feeling different to everybody else anymore, I just wanted to be alone for a while. But I knew they'd seen me through the window.

This wasn't common, it was far more likely I would be out all day with my friends, but the sadness was there like a tide: washing in and out for a few months at a time.

I would play guitar for hours on end at my friend's house, I loved watching stand-up comedy so there was still some joy in life. The bouts of low mood were shorter, less intense and with more distance between them, back then.

My memories of my childhood are largely happy and filled with all the good things. Like friends, balmy summer days and laughing.

I over compensated for this feeling of otherness. I became the class clown, I misbehaved. Whether I was doing it in school, at parties or for any possible excuse, I loved it.

I loved the attention and making people laugh. It made them want me to be there. It made me forget about feeling so separate from them. I would make cheap dirty jokes about sex and farts and annoy the teachers.

This was a coping mechanism I formed early and would cling to for most of my life. I was good at it. I could play everything off as a joke, so nothing bothered me.

If I made myself into someone people wouldn't like then when they didn't, that was my choice. As I grew older it became my default way of being.

I scalded myself for debasing myself like this and vowed never to do so again. I always did. I was quite spectacularly stung by this when, in an attempt to impress some teenagers at the skate-park, I downed a two-litre bottle of Cherryade they passed me. It had (unbeknown to me) been heavily laced with laxatives.

I spent several noisy hours grimacing, spasming, turning inside out on my friend's toilet and wishing toilet paper was softer and resolving to never to do anything like that again. (I did though.)

I feel I have to stress that my life was objectively a good one. We were well off and I never wanted for anything. I am incredibly lucky. Traumatic things have happened in my life and not caused me to become depressed. Relatives and pets have died. I fell out with friends, broke up with girlfriends, all the normal things that happen in most people's lives… and I've coped with them fine.

There was no reason for my illness, even though I thought there had to be. I know now that depression isn't an inability to cope with life. I was coping with it fine. I still do. I have the best mother anybody could ever ask for (I know everybody says that, but I actually do). My two brothers and I had a good relationship and I was healthy. I was loved. I had friends I'd go to parties with, drink underage with, spent all night in the woods. There were girls I'd message on MSN (back when that was still a thing) and kiss in parks.

All in all, I had no idea why my mood would change for weeks at a time, it was just the way I was.

This all made it worse. I wanted some kind of defect. Some kind of reason to feel the way I did. But there wasn't one. Mental health wasn't really something I remember being discussed when I was younger.

Even when I studied psychology, I wasn't really aware of it being something that could affect 'normal people'. Still, despite that, even after all my years at university and my training as a doctor, I still didn't change my mind for a long time. Depression robbed me of insight and it was impossible to see I was ill. Instead, I viewed myself as weak.

In school I was more interested in making people laugh than studying. I got mainly Cs at GCSE but during A levels, I got my act together and went to Warwick University to study chemistry. The idea was to work for a big pharmaceutical company in some capacity.

My time at university was difficult for me. My mood was lower for longer periods and I barely slept some times. This had happened from time to time, for as long as I can remember, and I never thought anything of it.

It was just something that happened to people, right? The excitement of living away from home was sucked down a hole of fatigue from not sleeping.

All the exciting societies and experiences I wanted to try, I missed out on because I just didn't see the point. Looking back on that now, I can see that as a tremendous waste. I remember walking the softly lit artificial world of the campus at night. Walking around the lakes with their herons and water fowls and just watching them. Thinking how much simpler their lives were than my own. How it didn't matter to them if they didn't fit in. I had the business card for the helpline for students feeling depressed and I looked at it, often, but never called it.

Surely I can't be depressed?!

I just needed to 'Man up' and get over it.

Eventually these spells passed, as they always did. I just had to ride it out.

It wasn't all bad. I made friends and at times experienced genuine happiness.

I joined a band with my friends, and those sweaty student gigs we forced our friends to go to, meant everything to me. Music was the light which managed to burn away the dark cloud of my depression.

We went to Manchester to play gigs. Playing pubs and clubs around the university, battle of the bands, arts festivals even earning a bit of money. It was fantastic! The guys in the band and me got on so well! This was it. I was enjoying things, looking forward to the future! Even sleeping! The shadow of depression had been lifted.

But during my final year it reared its ugly head again. Not suddenly and recognisably. But gradually. The tide was coming back in. My temporary happiness had just coincided with it being out.

It started with not doing the things I enjoyed because I couldn't be bothered. Then reminding myself that 'I probably should' – but not being able to bring myself to do them. Being 'tired' wasn't some creative thing like some people think. It's hell. I would sleep all day and still be just as tired. Then I couldn't sleep as much. Then I couldn't sleep at all. And my mood was so low. I wasn't enjoying band practices or gigs. Nothing had changed. For no reason, I was just numb all the time. More so than I had ever been. I couldn't concentrate. I was unpleasant to be around.

Lashing out at the people who cared most about me, and there were a lot of people who did care for me, who I treated poorly. I just couldn't figure out what the point in my existence was. If there was no joy in my life, what was the point?

But no suicidal thoughts. Not yet.

I managed to graduate with a first, even though in the end I was constantly low. I spent time looking for that thing which could make me happy: projects, my band, socialising, earning money, girls. Anything and everything to just try and squeeze one ounce of enjoyment from life. My interest in each one was fleeting, as I would jump from one thing to another trying to find happiness.

None of it helped. I never finished a project I started and rarely followed through on plans I had made.

I just hadn't found the 'right thing' yet. That had to be the problem. What I really needed was a purpose. I couldn't see the point in anything because I hadn't found out what my point was.

I needed to find what the point in me was.

The university I went to had a medical school. It was literally up on a hill all on its own, above everybody else. You would see the medical students with their hoodies, advertising their intellect and virtue walking around. Becoming a doctor wasn't really a life-long dream for me like it is for some people. When I thought about becoming one after seeing the medical students, I became infatuated with the idea. I thought of doctors as being some way different to everyone else. Intellectual, caring, people. Surely this was it!

I could finally justify my existence by being a doctor. I genuinely felt that the best thing a person could do was to help other people. I'd get to apply my love of science, make the world a bit better and live a comfortable life.

So if I could do that, I'd have found a purpose. And having a purpose would let me be happy… right?

To help with my application for medical school I got a job in a care home for people with dementia. Looking back, it was an awful job, sometimes we wouldn't even have enough disposable gloves and on night shifts I would be relegated to the laundry room.

Between changing soiled beds and making cups of tea I would have to wash all the residents' clothes. I was terrified at first. Having to wash people and feed them. But over time I got the hang of it and quite soon began to enjoy it. I built relationships with these wonderful people, and felt I genuinely improved their lives not by simply being there and doing a job, but by what I brought to the job. By being patient, understanding and thorough. My ability to make people laugh turned from a self-debasing habit in to a way to make these peoples days just a little bit brighter.

I was committed to this path now. Helping people, using my mind and incredibly, looking after people, it seemed to fit my personality.

I was made to be a doctor, I thought. I'm smart and like looking after people. Everything will be OK when I'm a doctor.

In the meantime, I carried on looking after the residents of the care home. I even used to buy them clothes with my own money when their families didn't. (Until the care home eventually told me to stop.)

This was where I discovered working nights. Here I could earn money and study! So this is what I did. Monday to Friday was university. Friday and Saturday night I would work so I could study and earn money. Sunday afternoon was for fun. Any more was a luxury.

After a while I got a job in a mental health hospital looking after dementia patients where I did the same thing. I would often go from waking up at six am on a Friday morning to going to bed at ten pm on a Sunday with three or four hours sleep in between. I was proud of that.

Then, the day I got into medical school coincided with a period of low mood.

I can't say I was genuinely happy with getting in. More relieved. It seemed like a step forward in a plan rather than an achievement. My hard work and sacrifice had paid off and I was going to do something which gave my life a purpose. I was setting out on the road to happiness. This was everything I had wanted and worked for.

I threw myself fully in to medical school. I was going to be a surgeon. One of the best. If it took twenty-three hours of work a day and one hour a day to eat and sleep then that's what I'd do.

I never felt the pride I expected to feel at being a medical student. I never bought a hoodie, I never got involved in societies or really made friends. I wanted to. But I didn't even like me! Why would they? I just felt so alienated from everybody. Feeling as though they belonged there and I didn't.

Throughout medical school I maintained my crude sense of humour. Wearing it was a suit of armour. It worked well. In short interactions, people didn't mind me, but they'd tire of me quickly and I'd be able to keep them at a distance.

The first set of exams at medical school I excelled in. After that, as my periods of time under the shadow of depression become longer, its cover denser and reach farther, I became an 'average' Medical student.

And I was dissatisfied with this. As if being an 'average' medical student wasn't good enough. This is just one of the many things I look back on and wonder if it was my ego or my depression. I can't blame all of my shortcomings on my mental health problems. Regardless, this turned in to an internal monologue of self-chastisement and comparing myself to others.

I stopped playing music as much. Only working on things, like the gym, which would 'improve me'. There were other people in medical school, high level athletes, people in the army, parents, and genuine geniuses.

Why wasn't I like that?

There is an attitude you will find commonly amongst medical students, doctors and other high achieving people, though it is certainly not limited to them.

It's one of venerating working, particularly at the detriment of your own health and social life. And I quickly and completely fell in to this trap. I treated rest as a luxury and socialising as something I didn't really need to do because it didn't help me achieve my goals.

This pressure to work and succeed was all consuming. You are surrounded by similar people and don't get a second to look from the outside in at just how pathological your behaviour is. It's not just doctors. Anybody can fall in to this trap. The more you work, the more virtuous you are.

I was proud when my family and friends would comment on how hard I work. Of course, it is a good thing to do, but it was all I did. I was comparing myself to other people who were behaving just as unhealthily as I was.

Medical school was competitive. Learning to draw the brachial plexus before your classmates, or being the owner of some obscure bit of knowledge the consultant would be impressed by on the ward round was a source of smug satisfaction. I know the times I had the answers that others didn't, I felt smug. I was surrounded by Type A personalities and workaholics and it normalised this destructive behaviour.

In my second year of medical school, I suffered with the worst bout of depression yet. There wasn't a precipitant, I can remember just a slow and insidious descent. This was accompanied by melancholy and self-loathing. It ended with an inability to find joy in anything, insomnia and irritability. It was familiar, so in a sick kind of way it was comfortable.

The environment of medical school seemed to make things worse. Not giving myself time to come up for air as I drowned in the workload I placed on myself. I didn't know I had depression at the time I just assumed it was normal.

I started committing very minor acts of self-harm. Nothing anybody would notice. I wouldn't even leave a mark. They were just to punish myself. I didn't even know what I was being punished for.

Small things: like turning on the iron and seeing how long I could keep my hand on it. Cutting the inside of my thighs where nobody would see. Digging keys in to my head to draw blood at night when I couldn't sleep.

The clearest memory I have of this episode is of sobbing in the kitchen in front of my family. My head bowed. Just trying to articulate what the problem was. But I couldn't.

I don't know if it's naive of me to think that this is the only time they knew something was wrong. Surely there wasn't a problem. I was passing all my exams, had friends and hobbies. I was just sad. Everybody got sad sometimes. It was normal. I would get up, carry on and smile.

I needed to work harder. That was the problem. I would go to medical school all week and work Friday and Saturday night shifts. Nobody had the slightest clue about how I was feeling except my family, and eventually that, too, passed.

I stayed in medical school. I had good grades, graduated and moved to Wales to start my career.

Chapter Three
Freshly Pressed Doctor

I didn't know anybody in Wales.

I didn't know much about Wales. I knew they liked rugby, disliked the English, and that if you got a dozen or so elderly Welsh men in the same room, they would spontaneously form an all-male voice choir. I thought too much had happened in Coventry.

I had lived in Coventry my whole life, and, as such, every bad thing I had experienced had been experienced there. I wanted to leave it behind.

But some things, it seems, you can't outrun and the problem with your shadow is that it follows you wherever you go. There's no outrunning that.

I lived in hospital accommodation, a tall block with a ten foot by twelve-foot room, a single bed older than me, half a shelf in a fridge (The person with which I had shared that shelf with had a very liberal definition of the word half).

The showers had peeling paint and rusty fittings. I shared a floor with eleven other people and two of them I would go on to become quite good friends with. As well as a consultant who seemed to reserve his loudest conversations while only wearing what must've been a hand towel when getting out of the shower for the common room.

I did not become friends with them.

But I was here. A freshly pressed doctor! I had just driven here in my new ford fiesta I had treated myself to when I qualified.

I remember seeing the "Welcome to Wales" sign on the bright sunny day as I drove there and the thrill it gave me. My life packaged in the boot and on my back seat, armed with my knowledge of anatomy, physiology, biochemistry, pathology, some psychology, models of consultations, examination techniques, and some rudimentary x-ray interpretation skills.

I was going to be the hardest working, most impressive first year doctor (F1) ever. I would go the extra mile for my patients. I would be kind no matter what, be thorough and safe. No patient would be in pain for long, no diagnosis missed, none of my colleagues would have to re-write my drug charts or dose my warfarin on the weekend. My seniors would see all of this and reward me with training opportunities usually reserved for doctors one or even two years ahead of me. People would be glad I was there and I would do the best for my patients. I would be helping people because that's all I had ever wanted to do. On top of this I would do audits, write papers, teach medical students, go on Christmas nights out and spend my rare but hard-won days off with all the new friends I would make in my job.

Maybe even at the beach or the rugby. I was awash in unrealistic optimism.

But after living without any for so long, I was drunk on it.

My first job was in paediatric surgery. I still remember my first day. A mixture of inductions, meeting the foundation program directors and my new colleagues. Consultants, nurses and ward clerks.

Every newly qualified doctor in the country starts on what is known as 'black Wednesday'. This wasn't going to be a black Wednesday for me. This was the first day of the rest of my life, and I was going to make a good account of myself. I walked on to the ward my stethoscope around my neck and my freshly procured bleep sat proudly on my belt. It meant more to me than a world title belt would have.

I made it. I was finally a doctor. I was introduced to everybody on the ward and began working. I quickly realised that as much as I knew about what was written in the text books, I knew very little about actually being a doctor.

Sometimes when you take blood from very young babies, you will perform a prick with a spring-loaded needle on their heel or toe. Then with skill and patience you can collect this, send it to the lab, diagnose your patient and save the day. It took me several attempts over two weeks to get this right. To have enough blood to fill a bottle. There was a mountain of lightly blood-stained cotton wool and a pair of very polite, but obviously dubious parents, as well as a very annoyed eight-month-old.

I sent it to the lab, pleased with myself and the results came back. The sample had been handled roughly and the cells had split. The results were useless. The very experienced nurse practitioner (a highly trained and skilled nurse who can do everything a doctor in their first few years can do… only better) swiftly, painlessly and professionally collected a sample, calmed mum and dad and left me dumbstruck. They then taught me how to do it properly.

A good nurse practitioner (and there are a lot of them) is more use than a good many junior doctors. As is a good nurse, healthcare assistant, physio, OT, pharmacist. Even the catering assistant has saved a life.

Like the one who stopped me being murdered by my consultant for being the only one to notice that if this patient was going for an operation, "Maybe they shouldn't eat a Sunday roast just before doctor?"

My optimism quickly took a hit when I realised the realities of being an F1. I was a secretary who could prescribe drugs and take blood. Occasionally I got to go to theatre and hold a retractor while being asked questions I didn't know the answer to. So I started reading up on the anatomy and procedure of the operations the night before. Even watching YouTube videos of them so I knew the steps.

They just asked harder questions or called me a swat. This wasn't universal and some people were very nice and patient. They provided me opportunities and taught me. I would stay late every now and then but not all that often. There wasn't really a need.

But when I did, I just thought, "Good job I live on site," and was proud of myself for being committed to my calling. I stuck to my old trick of hiding behind humour and cockiness. I remember one time telling the nurses on the ward not to worry because "I was here now" like the hero I wanted to be.

It was meant as a joke. I knew that I wasn't much use. And I knew they knew. I thought they knew I knew. But I wanted to try and be part of the team. They looked at me as if they'd just watched me be sick in somebody's mouth while they yawned.

Aside from stresses from your own team there are a multitude of other small cruelties and inconveniences you have to deal with. On a ward round it may be decided that a patient needs a certain scan. It might be a CT scan or an ultrasound. It is then often the F1s job to go and request this. It can be a nerve-wracking experience. You discuss the request with a radiologist and some of them are very nice and ask helpful questions and might even teach you. Some aren't as nice. At times they wouldn't even turn around to say hello. They would extend their hand up and snatch the form from you.

This is another part of the job which has helped suck the motivation out of many junior doctors.

"I didn't make this decision," I replied, once to a particularly surly line of questioning, "My consultant did. Maybe you should talk to them."

Without looking back the radiologist replied, "But I can't take my frustration out on them, can I?"

In their first two years doctors rotate every four months. When I moved to adult general surgery I began staying late. Everybody did. I should have worked 8 till 5. There were on calls and night shifts of course and everyone had to do their share it wasn't a problem.

It is necessary for a safe and effective health service to have it staffed twenty-four hours a day. I would often finish at eight pm. I would sometimes still be there when the night shift came on after not having eaten all day. The team I was working with was fantastic and we all supported each other, with juniors from other teams helping out when they could and people making sure we got home.

Sometimes the only thing I would eat all day were the spoils of a covert-raid, stealing a biscuit or two from the kitchen. Which, the ward sister wide-eyed with rage told me I was absolutely not allowed to do. After tax, student loans and pension my take home rate from this job was just a bit lower than minimum wage.

I absolutely loved it. I loved that I could get a cannula in when one of my colleagues couldn't (and if you're reading this you know who you are. And, yes, I am going to keep bringing it up). I especially loved theatre. The patient would enter this room with a potentially life-threatening problem such as a bowel obstruction or a tumour and after the administrations of the surgeon and anaesthetist and the help of everybody in the room they left without it!

It was just the best thing a human being could do in my eyes. I started going to theatre as often as I could. Staying even later. Practicing the art of retraction, hoping that I would be allowed to do a hand tie or use the diathermy or put the ports in. I made sure my sutures were the neatest and memorised the names of the instruments on the scrub nurse's trolley as they were passed on to the surgeon.

In my second year as a doctor, I had a job in A&E. The same A&E which has been described by people who have worked in as, "Being more stressful than a war zone," The rota was awful. I began with one week of solid twelve-hour shifts. Ten am till ten pm. Luckily there weren't any windows in the department, so you didn't have any concept of daylight or time of day anyway. So I didn't really miss it.

But it didn't stop there! One in three weekends. Plus night shifts... I loved it. I was independently diagnosing and treating patients. I was exposed to so much medicine and learning so much. And in terms of practical procedures, it easily rivalled surgery in my mind. Stitching a wound, femoral nerve blocks, and fracture manipulation.

I could even stop those giant spots from going to the surgeons by draining them myself in the department! The satisfaction from draining a golf ball sized collection six-month-old cottage cheese is one of the more perverse joys doctors experience. Sometimes members of staff will even come in to watch the big ones if the patients let us.

A&E was so varied and wide ranging. I got involved and made sure that foundation doctors had dedicated time in the paediatric and rhesus areas of the department so that they felt more comfortable when they had to work out there for hours with less staff. I made friends with the nurses and secretaries and caterers and cleaners. It was great. In my mind for the first time, I felt like a doctor, and even a little bit like I belonged.

Much has been written about the pressures A&E is under by more informed and more intelligent people than me. All I can tell you that is that they're all true. I can also tell you that every single person working in that department is tired, stressed, hungry, thirsty and needs a wee. On top of that, before coming to assess your sprained ankle, the condition you wanted to get checked out 'Just to be safe' or alcohol with or without drug overdose, they might have been involved in a failed paediatric resuscitation, as in, literally just seen a child die. Can you imagine seeing a child die and then having to go back to work? The vast majority of patients are understanding, calm and appreciative.

Some frustration is only natural and we're all frustrated that you have to wait. We want to provide you with the best care. Nobody works in health care for any other reason.

There's no money in it, it takes a huge toll on your life and is proven to be bad for your health. We do it because we want to care for people and it can even be fun sometimes.

But the abusive drunks, the patient who threatened to punch my nursing colleague in her, "Fat fucking face," for not seeing to his daughter's hay fever... The student who vomited on my shoes and then told me to, "Fuck off."

Well, they made the job less fun. Despite all this I really felt at home there and I felt more useful than I did in surgery.

After my first two years as a doctor (known as F1 and F2) I decided to be a locum for a year or "F3" as it is colloquially known. A Locum is a doctor who fills in shortages that the hospital has and isn't in a training post. Instead, they are providing a service. This is the light at the end of the foundation tunnel for some doctors.

Here you can choose your hours, and because you work filling in gaps in a rota, often at short notice. You are not guaranteed work but you are paid more per hour. Finally, having money and time you can reap the rewards of all those hours of study, the nights out you missed with friends because you had an exam, and the sunny days you watched as a prisoner from the library because you were working on a project.

Luckily the newspapers have informed you all about how we are bleeding the NHS dry in doing this. So, I'm sure you're all fully aware. It's almost certainly got nothing to with the fact that the NHS would collapse without them and that without the higher wages on offer, people wouldn't do these jobs because they're so awful. The irony that the reward for the job you've worked so hard for, for so many years is that you have to do it, less while being lambasted in the media isn't lost on me.

I had a job picking up shifts in A&E. There are always shifts in A&E. They don't have enough trainees because the job is tough and the rota tougher. So I worked, I worked a lot. I don't think I remember turning down a shift. But when I did book time off, I went on holidays, bought a nice car, and rented a nice house with my friend.

I was treated well and I think I was liked within the department. Most importantly, I was practicing good medicine. I could work in resus on my own and the consultants seemed to trust me and liked having me there.

But one day without any reason it was just a bit harder to get out of bed, I would get just a bit less enjoyment out of whatever I was doing. Just a bit more rumination than normal. I carried on. I didn't even notice, really, and in its cunning way depression wore me down like a tide erodes a cliff.

Recently a former doctor has written a mildly successful book some of you may have heard of or even read. In it, they share their worst day.

My worst day was coming at the worst time. I had spent the morning lying in bed, face down, feeling low after a night of minimal sleep. But I got up and went in for the afternoon shift. I was so tired that on the ten-minute walk in to work my legs were aching and I could hardly lift my head.

A patient had come in by ambulance and we got on well. They were a very pleasant elderly gentlemen, and in the ten or fifteen minutes we spent together as I took a history, examined them and formulated a plan, and we had made each other laugh. The whole consultation had a relaxed feel to it. I used some of my stock jokes to great effect. I mistook their wife for their daughter and as I slapped their hand to bring up the veins, I told them that beating patients was a, "Perk of the job."

The patient laughed and told me it was nice to have a doctor with a personality.

They had vomited at home and had some abdominal pain after eating fish and chips. The vomit was described to me as bright yellow and the pain in the right upper quadrant of the abdomen going through to the back and the shoulder. The heart rate, blood pressure and other vital signs were all normal. They were sat up, appeared pain free and very well.

I'm sure every doctor reading this is screaming at the book: "It's gallstones!"

However, the patient also had several risk factors for vascular problems. I took some blood, ordered some tests, gave some painkillers and went to see another patient while the lab processed my requests.

On the way, I mentioned the patient to my registrar (a senior doctor) and they were going to come and scan the patient's abdomen to be sure there wasn't anything unexpected. The patient suddenly experienced severe abdominal pain and the blood pressure dropped. I called my senior registrar who performed an ultrasound scan of the abdomen. The patients' aorta (which is the biggest artery in the body) was leaking.

This was identified within fifteen to twenty minutes of them being in the department. We took them to resus, the area in A&E for the sickest patients and spoke to the surgeons as quickly as we could. Despite our best efforts the patient died.

Everybody was very nice to me.

"It wasn't your fault."

"You acted as quickly as you could."

"Nobody else would have done anything differently," said my colleagues.

"Yes, it is your fault, you got the diagnosis wrong, any other doctor would have seen this," said my mind.

The head of the department even spoke to me in a cubicle which is a big deal. Because sacrificing an A&E cubicle in a busy department is enough to make the nurse in charge liable to commit murder.

Even if you're only sacrificing it for the amount of time it takes to comfort a junior doctor who is convinced he has killed a patient. They were supportive and professional and acted as consultants should.

The family was upset. If 'upset' is even the right word for how you'd feel in their situation, but they didn't blame me. I felt it important to speak to them because we'd built a relationship. But it never left me, that if I was just a bit better, and bit smarter, that person might not have died and that family might not be thinking about funerals.

It turns out nobody was pointing the finger at me but myself.

After a cup of tea, I went back to work. I carried that burden, self-imposed or not, with me throughout the rest of the shift and have done ever since.

I don't think this incident caused me to become depressed. I was becoming depressed anyway but now I had another big reason for myself loathing and the poisoned part of my mind latched on to it. It was turning it into fuel for its self-destructive fire.

As I began to become aware of my low mood, I thought I was working too much. It was telling that in old cards from my girlfriend for birthdays, Christmas etc… she would always mention how hard I worked and that she was proud of me for it. I wanted more time for my hobbies so I eased off the shifts.

Playing the guitar had been my favourite thing to do since I first picked one up. But every time I picked one up, I'd strum a few chords and grow tired of it. There was no enjoyment in it any more. I couldn't see the point in it. I couldn't concentrate on books, television, listening to music, anything at all. My mood was low and I craved silence. I had trouble sleeping.

I'd had had trouble sleeping before, but not like this. I would wake up at five am regardless of what time I went to bed and sleeping through the night was becoming more and more rare. Then it became harder to fall asleep. I was tired, but the more tired I was the less I was sleeping.

I had no joy in life. I was eating to excess and putting on weight. Depression had once again imperceptibly crept up on me, sinking its fangs deeper in to me than ever before.

And now, the one thing which I thought excused my miserable existence, turns out I wasn't very good at. Nothing could break through this constant fog of melancholy I was living in. But I had everything! Good job, money, friends, health, girlfriend. Why wasn't I happy? Was something wrong with me? Would I always be like this?

It was this time that I first seriously considered suicide.

I can remember it well. It was by no means my first suicidal thought, I'm sure everybody has had at least one in their life, but it was the first time I acted on it.

Somebody had jumped to their death from the top floor of the hospital multi story the year before. So one night, after lying in bed for a few hours and not sleeping, I walked the ten minutes to the hospital. Climbed the grey concrete steps that somebody had took the liberty of pissing in to the top floor.

I just stood there for a while. Felt the cold wind on my face and through the thin fabric of my t-shirt. I don't know if I went there to kill myself or just to try and feel something. I was so numb. I couldn't bare it. The sky was cloudless and dark punctured by pin pricks of golden and white light. The moon was a picturesque crescent. There was a cold, fine rain in the air. Almost like a mist, and it soothed my skin and my mind as I stood there taking deep measured breaths through my nose.

I still wasn't sure why I was there, really. I am terrified of heights. I have been known to glare menacingly at small children who think that escalators are for playing on and not for gripping tightly, hyperventilating and praying for it to be over.

But I wasn't scared that night. I walked to the edge, and lifted myself up over it looking down. I wanted to be frightened, to feel terror as I looked down. I didn't. Instead I imagined the dark wet grey of the pavement rushing to meet me, splitting my skull and forcing its contents out of my ears and through the base of my skull. My weight colliding with the floor destroying my facial bones, popping my eyes like stepped on grapes, crushing cervical vertebrae and ruining whatever else was left at the mercy of the impact of the fall.

I wondered if anybody from A&E would recognise me. (I'd not taken any ID with me so they wouldn't.)

But the thought of my family, and the knowledge that this episode like all the others would pass, stopped me.

It was odd how I felt no fear at the thought of dying. Six months ago, I had been happy and enjoying my life. But now I wanted to die. All it would have taken was the energy it takes to lean forward and I would have been free of it, and felt nothing.

I couldn't do it.

I made a compromise with myself. Endure. If it stayed like this you could kill yourself because you've given it your all. I would have tried to get over it, to live on and if I failed, suicide was an ever-present option.

It was almost comforting to know that it was always there for me. Like a spy carrying a cyanide capsule in case of prolonged torture in the face of capture. I had suicide in case of prolonged torture in the face of life.

I bought a large bottle of fizzy pop and over the course of a few weeks placed about two hundred crushed paracetamols in there. Taped it up in heavy silver electrical tape. Wrote, 'way out' on it in big, thick black marker pen and hid it in the cupboard behind my desk in a suitcase.

It soothed me, knowing it was always there. That I could drink it all at night, when nobody was in, and that would be it.

I also knew that paracetamol overdose was a nasty way to die. There was liver failure, pain and excessive bleeding. But I didn't care. That was a more attractive option to me than living. If I couldn't enjoy my hobbies, it was probably because they were stupid. If I was dissatisfied in my life, it's because I hadn't done enough to put myself where I needed to be.

For one last chance at life, I threw myself into work.

It provided distraction for a while, I presented some research at a conference which went well. I was becoming confident in my abilities as a doctor especially in A&E.

I finally got what I wanted, I was autonomous, helping people. I put chest drains in people and watched blood pour out, allowing them to breathe again. I reassured parents that there was nothing wrong with their children and sent them on their way smiling when they had come in anxious.

I treated fits, put dislocated shoulders back in to place, taught medical students and tried my best to stay happy and make the department a nicer place to work. I would buy bags of sweets and put them in all the different areas of A&E for people, especially on night shifts, just to try and make the shift more tolerable for everyone.

They'd never know, that the day after nearly throwing myself off a multi-story car park, I was buying sweets to try and cheer people up.

The perception that I was helping people, using my skills and seemed to be good at it was everything to me and I think it means an awful lot to most doctors.

But, inevitably, over time the tide was coming in. It drowned my mind again in its cold, dark waters. Every other aspect of my life began to matter less until eventually even being a doctor didn't matter. It was an exceptionally cruel part of the disease, to strip meaning after I had been so close to finding it.

To ruin something, I had worked so hard for. Something I had been pinning all my hopes on.

There was one day in A&E, which in hindsight, was a sign of just how numb I was. A young undiagnosed type one diabetic came in with diabetic keto acidosis as a result of very high blood sugars and a lack of insulin. Because they hadn't been diagnosed as diabetic, they hadn't been treated and presented with a quite severe complication. It's not that much of a rare way for new diabetics to present itself. The blood had become acidotic, potassium became raised, which could put the heart in to a very dangerous rhythm.

It was not quite critical yet but the patient had the potential to become severely unwell. Luckily, by replacing the insulin, hydrating the patient and correcting the electrolyte imbalances the patient recovered quite quickly. Blood tests showed me that the pH is improving, the blood sugar coming down and potassium normalising.

But as this patient's mother thanked me from behind mascara-streaked eyes for saving their child's life, I was indifferent. Annoyed even! This conversation was taking too long. I had other patients to see.

That is not the person I am, nor the person I want to be.

It was the person depression was turning me in to. I was irritable, miserable, and hated being at work. Of course at the time I didn't realise it. I thought it was due to A&E not being the right fit for me. So I left to work in surgery in the hope that my problems were because of where I was working.

I never even thought I could have a problem.

I was lucky enough to get a long-term post in a department I really liked. However, I had already agreed to some night shifts at another hospital. I would do my night shifts then go over to the other hospital for the morning ward round. Then go home and sleep.

I thought I was providing continuity of care for my patients and support for my juniors as well. This only lasted for about a month, and it wasn't every day but even the driving was unsafe, let alone making decisions about patients.

Luckily, they were all checked by the seniors and to my knowledge I didn't make any mistakes. I wasn't asked to do this but it's what was expected. Not explicitly by any one person, but implicitly by the culture.

In retrospect, I was becoming more and more depressed and depriving myself of sleep because I wanted to fit in with the surgical culture. It was a perfect storm.

This was the first time I recognised working so hard might be damaging.

In my mind, I had an agreement with each hospital and I would fulfil it. It was never about the money and it wasn't forever. I could cope.

However, my lack of concentration was bleeding into my work. I thought it was because I was tired so I stopped doing nights and tried to sleep more. But that didn't help. I became anxious about every decision I made and checked everything at least twice. Worrying that I was just too stupid to be able to notice things and remember them as quickly as everybody else.

Some days I would get in to work an hour early to get ready for the ward round so I didn't seem slow or stupid on it. I lied and told my housemate I went to the gym at five am because it was quiet. But it was an excuse to leave the house early after a night of not sleeping, and to check my work again.

This was just one of the multiple lies I told people to hide my depression. Lies I told myself as well.

My girlfriend, a qualified nurse (I love a cliche as much as the next doctor) and I wanted to do something nice for her.

Since I was working so much and had some savings, I decided a holiday was the right way to go. At a restaurant, I gave her a tablet with a list of the places we were going.

I had tried to be romantic and had one destination on each page. She scrolled down with what appeared to be a never-ending list of destinations, Rome, Venice, Prague, Budapest, Berlin, Amsterdam, then on to Thailand. A four-week holiday to see the world with the woman I loved.

It should have been perfect. It's the dream. She cried on the way home. She told me it was the best day of her life and she didn't want it to end.

To be sat, two feet away from somebody experiencing such joy, while I felt like my mind was rotting, was awful.

The distance between us could be measured in inches but I had never felt so far away.

I don't really remember too much of the holiday. Some parts of it I did enjoy. But most of it was just covered by that cloud. I don't think I let on to my girlfriend. It would have ruined her holiday. We did everything you could want, nice meals, history, art, cocktails, and shopping. On paper and social media, it was perfect.

But one night, at the top of a skyscraper in Bangkok drinking expensive whiskey, I just couldn't get rid of the urge to throw myself off.

I applied for training jobs in A&E and surgery, but couldn't bring myself to go to the interview. The anxiety I felt at a potential rejection was enormous.

"You weakling. It's a good job you didn't go. Even if you did manage to trick them into giving you a job, you'd just be taking the space of somebody who'd deserves it more."

So I didn't go. And to be honest, I just didn't care. I quite wanted to not have a job. To be fired. To have everything taken away from me. I didn't deserve it, because I didn't appreciate it. I knew I was competent in both specialities and I had a good CV.

But I also knew I wasn't good enough. So I kept on working as a Locum in various departments. Leaving the big hospital I had been in to work in a smaller one.

Reading back over what I have just written, I can see how absolutely mental it is to think you can work constantly and not sleep.

How I viewed, what I see is now text-book depression, as my own inability to cope with tasks and situations which everybody else found easy.

But that's exactly how I had lived since medical school.

The pattern of mood fluctuations continued.

Eighteen months of depression with six months off.

I thought it was just how I would live until one day I'd kill myself.

Chapter Four
Getting Worse

After going travelling and not attending my interviews, I had been a doctor for four years. My mood was becoming worse still. I just couldn't snap out of it this time.

I lost six months of my life to a routine of misery. No joy, no hope. But on the outside, I was fully functioning, sociable and happy. I was very good at hiding it from people. I was working in the surgical department of a small hospital. Still doing my job, and doing it well. Still dreading going home and dreading the night times even more. I had been trying my best to cope but just not managing.

I thought the holiday was going to be the reset button I needed. But it didn't work. If I couldn't be happy sipping cocktails on a tropical island, then when could I be? Happiness wasn't even something I could remember any more.

So I went back to work.

I was walking down a hospital corridor. I had driven to work fantasising about a tire blow out or head-on collision after another night of not sleeping. There were floor to ceiling windows on my right, bombarding me with sterile white light from behind mountains of dense cloud.

I was so tired that turning my head to look at it hurt my eyes. Wards full of sick and dying people were on my left. There, in the middle, my mind raced.

Suicide consumed me. The pressure in my head was building. When you go to the cinema before the movie starts there is an advert for the sound system used. Usually a siren building in intensity until you fear you can't take it getting any louder. Then, mercifully it stops and the film starts. My suicidal thoughts were like this. A siren of ever-increasing intensity that I just couldn't ignore, and the volume kept building. It was relentless. The only way I could see to make it stop was to take my own life. It made any other thought impossible. You thought the intensity had to plateau but it kept on building.

If this is life… how can I stand it? I hadn't slept for three days. Nights were spent awake wishing I was asleep, or dead. There were no feelings in my life except pain, sadness and exhaustion. During the day everybody kept asking me if I was ok or telling me I looked miserable.

Always, reflexively, a joke back.

Usually one that had me as the subject of it.

"Yeah, I was up all night because I had hurt my wrist tripping over my penis in the shower," or some other juvenile retort.

The spiteful monologue was in full force. Stronger than it had ever been.

"Kill yourself you weakling. This is all you've got now, either making stupid jokes or being a shit doctor. Your family wouldn't even care anyway."

The sane part of me had been telling myself not to do it.

Day after day, the same corridor. The same harsh white light. The siren was battering the brittle defences of my sleep deprived mind.

I had spent the night worrying about my brother. He played rugby and I had heard a horror story about somebody being paralysed in a match. I lay awake in the dark, wondering if he was ever paralysed, would he want me to smother him with a pillow? And would I be able to?

I hated myself for being so selfish and worrying about how I would handle that situation.

"Yet again, you're making everything about you! Don't you think how hard this would be for him? Not everything is a narrative with you at the centre. They'd probably be better off without you."

The thought that maybe my family and friends would be better off without me burrowed into my mind from that moment on.

Maybe, by removing myself from the world, my family would be sad at first, but in the long run, their lives would be better.

How could I even think that about my brother? Even worse, how could I make it about me?

I was so selfish and twisted. No wonder everybody thought I was a joke. If I was better off dead or not was irrelevant. What was apparent to me now, was that the world would be better without me in it.

This thought festered as I walked silently around the hospital. Making radiology requests and being interrogated, being shouted at by infection control nurses because my sleeve was rolled up just below my elbow, not over it.

Being told the referral I had been told to make was inappropriate by the irate voice on the other end of the phone despite me not being the one who asked for it.

It extended its reach into every recess of my mind. Every facet of my day became a justification for the act. Every time I failed to take blood from a patient was my own inadequacy contributing to the mass of human suffering within the hospital.

Every comment was an insult. Every minor inconvenience a sign that I was not built for this world and that it had no obligation to keep me in it. I realised over the course of that day that killing myself wasn't selfish.

Staying alive was.

This realisation was met with relief. Finally I wouldn't have to continue with this suffering. Not only that, I would be helping people. Which is really all I have ever wanted to do.

"Quitter! No wonder you're taking the easy way out. This is why people will be better off without you."

Perversely, the fact that I was relieved by this made me hate myself even more. But I was numbed by exhaustion.

I drove home in silence that day. I walked in and my housemate told me I looked tired. I laughed, made another joke and told him that I was going to bed. I walked up my stairs and into my room. On the left was the en-suite. I walked in, careful not to look at the mirror on my left. I didn't want to see him. Instead, I looked up at the sky light.

Effortlessly, a plan came to me. I lay on my bed. All I wanted was peace. And now it was in sight. It was a foregone conclusion that I was going to die. My suffering, which was all because of my own selfishness and inadequacy, would be over. And with it, the ending of the burden my existence placed on others. I had to wait for my house mate to be out, and luckily he was going away the next day.

I spent the night without sleep. During that sleepless night I watched the clock waiting for 6am – when it was time to get out of bed.

I ruminated over how I wasn't worth the air that I breathed. That despite all my privilege, I was miserable. How I'd tried everything to make myself happy, and failed. How everybody thought of me as a joke. How my mother had two other children who were funny, intelligent, kind and handsome that she could be proud of. Then she had me. The weirdo who made the dirty jokes. The black sheep of the family. They'd be such a nice family without me.

They wouldn't have to try and include me in conversations around the dinner table at Christmas or pretend to be pleased to see me. I visualised the three of them: my mother and two brothers, around the dinner table, surrounded by conversation and laughter that flowed freely.

At work, I laughed with patients. A young patient had to have a mark in permanent pen drawn on them so we knew which side the operation should be on. I asked them if they'd like me to draw glasses or a moustache on them while they were asleep. The patient and the nurses laughed.

I made sure that all the medication they'd need after their operation was prescribed. Painkillers, anti-sickness medicine, drugs to stop blood clots. I put my hand on the patients shoulder and promised them that if I had to have the same operation, I would want this surgeon to be the one to do it. As soon as I left the curtain, my thoughts would return to what I was going to do that night.

I would rub my hand on my throat applying pressure to my windpipe trying to get used to it, so that I wouldn't panic. I did this while walking between wards. I did a lot of walking that day.

I felt the weight of the future lift from my shoulders as I wheeled my desk chair into my bathroom. Its hard plastic wheels rolled noisily on the tiles and reverberated around the room. I had definitely made the right decision in waiting to be alone.

"About time you did something right."

I stood on the chair and wound the large metal handle of the skylight shut and looked at the seal. It was thick wood, and closed tightly. I smiled my first genuine smile in weeks. This would work. I got down from the chair, walked in to my bedroom and opened up my wardrobe, pulling out a thick black belt. I threaded the strap through the buckle to make a loop and tied a knot at the long end. I wrapped this knot in silver electrical tape tightly and carefully. I couldn't afford any mistakes.

I climbed back up on the chair, opened the skylight, pushed the knot through and closed the skylight trapping the knot outside and the loop inside. I stepped down from the chair and looked up at my makeshift gallows. I grabbed the belt and hung from it to ensure it could take my weight. Not the smallest amount of movement. Not even a protesting creak from the ceiling.

If I only ever did one thing right, it would be this. It held my weight. I turned around, left the bathroom, being sure to close the door behind me, and sat down to write my suicide notes.

The notes were easy to write and cathartic.

"Nobody is even going to read these. Who gives a fuck why you're doing this? Just get it over with."

I spent about three hours apologising to my family and friends, reassuring them that they would understand. Explaining that I was doing this for them. Explaining why they were better off without me. Explaining how I had tried so hard to stay alive, to find some kind of happiness, some purpose. But I just couldn't find either.

I'm not sure how much of it I meant and how much I was writing because that seemed like what I should be writing. My hand flew across the paper. The black biro I was using was more use to the world than I was.

I detailed my character flaws: how I had wasted opportunities. How everything that had been given to me should have been given to someone else, and how now they could all move on with their lives without me holding them back.

I started to feel as if I was on the right path. I was pleased at the prospect of an end to the way I had been feeling. While I wrote, I was drinking whiskey from a glass I had been given by my best friend when they asked me to be their daughters godfather.

I didn't need a drink for Dutch courage. I stopped before I was drunk. I wanted to be present for this.

"If it's painful, you deserve it."

I wanted to make sure I felt every bit of it. After all the notes were written, and placed into envelopes with names carefully written on, I stood up to die.

We tend to see ourselves as the protagonists of our own heroic narratives. Movies and books have taught us that every event is significant, every sacrifice noble and every victory glorious. We apply this logic to ourselves relentlessly.

As such, you would expect your own death to be the most momentous of events. Every faucet should be unique to you, your favourite song playing in the background. Wearing the suit you were married in. Slitting your wrists with the pen knife your grandfather used in the war. Everything with a meaning.

I was under no such illusion. I intended to see my life extinguished hanging at the end of a cheap belt for no cause other than to put an end to the misery I was enduring and inflicting on others.

For the first time, in as long as I can remember, I had hope. There was light at the end of the tunnel. I hoped for oblivion. Peace. Whether it was that, or the pearly gates, or the gaping maw containing unspeakable horror… it was irrelevant. I would be free of the relentless pressure I experienced every moment of every day.

I looked at myself in the mirror. My reflection and I glared at each other with loathing.

Deep down, in the pit of my consciousness the small, sane part of me screamed at me to stop. I thought this was the weakness in me trying to talk me out of what I had to do. My weakness had robbed me of everything else… The joy in my life. My relationship. My sleep. My purpose and any hope for the future. I would be damned if it robbed me of my last chance to do the right thing.

My reflection and I steeled our wills and climbed up on to the chair. There was no trembling in my legs. No rapid breathing or palpitations, just a comforting knowledge of impending tranquillity. I put my head through the loop of the belt and pulled it tight around my neck. Turned to face the door and looked down at my bare feet on the black surface of the chair.

I jumped.

There was no slowing of time. My life did not flash before my eyes and I had no regrets about what I was doing.

The belt pulled tight around my neck, closing my windpipe completely. Crushing my veins and arteries in the side of my neck. It all came on quicker than I could have imagined. My eyes bulged and veins distended.

I fought the urge to lift my hands up and pull at my neck. This was my final exercise of will power, and it was the most important, beneficial thing I would ever do for myself and others. I panicked.

The small reserves of oxygen in my blood were used up and with the rising carbon dioxide I couldn't exhale creating an urge to breathe which became irresistible.

I began to kick my legs, but I kept my hands down. Just as panic began to overtake me, a blackness creeped in-to the peripheries of my vision.

I plummeted down from my belt to the floor.

Initially, my disappointment was over ridden by me greedily sucking in mouthfuls of air as I reached up and felt the belt around my neck.

Back to the mirror as I retched and cough over the sink. Those eyes that I hated were red and watering. I pulled the end of the belt from around my neck and looked at it.

It had ripped and given way, along the extra slit I had made in it with a kitchen knife after I had lost weight since my appetite had deserted me.

I doubled over and let out a shout. There was a pain in my throat and I began to cough.

"I can't even die properly! Pathetic! Weak! Stupid! And now I have to go on living, feeling like this. With the added knowledge that I can't even kill myself."

I was a failure. The only important thing I had ever done, and I had failed. I grabbed two handfuls of my hair and pulled, and let out another shout before another fit of coughing.

The disappointment I felt at having to continue living was, even now, the strongest emotion I have ever felt. I sat down on the cold tile floor of the bathroom and cried.

Great shuddering sobs wracked my body as I dug my finger nails in to my head and pulled my hair. It was the first time I had cried since I had been feeling like this.

I don't know how long I sat there doing that. But I longed for an end to it. I have never wanted to hurt somebody as much as I wanted to hurt myself that night.

I have never hated anybody as much as I hated the weak fool that failed his solitary, important task.

I frantically thought of other ways to kill myself. There were plenty of knives in the kitchen, I thought about rushing downstairs, opening the drawer and repeatedly stabbing myself in the abdomen but was worried it wouldn't kill me.

I had been in enough laparotomies and fashioned enough stomas myself to know that there was no guarantee of hitting some vital conduit. And even if I did, there was no guarantee that it would kill me.

I thought about an overdose, but if I ended up on ITU I could end up a prisoner in my own body without the option of suicide.

A hosepipe to the exhaust of my car was a possibility… but it was early in the evening and other people might see my car. I'd had a drink and didn't want to drive in case I hurt somebody other than myself.

I had been weak and stupid.

I would not fail again.

As I thought about all this, I was gripped by an iron resolve.

What little strength I had would not fail me now.

Chapter Five
Suicide Round Two

That night I stayed awake, carefully formulating my plan and carrying out the first few steps.

It was a welcome break from the nightly torment of wishing for sleep, and being denied it. I shouldn't be sleeping, anyway, because I had things to think about and bed wasn't a place for serious thinking.

I sat at my desk next to my neat pile of suicide notes and jotted down several ideas under the soft yellow glow of my desk lamp.

I had been rash and stupid. I knew a lot about the human body and how it worked and I hadn't used that to my advantage.

This time I would succeed.

As far I was concerned, I was already dead. I just hadn't killed myself yet.

I chose a knife from the kitchen. It was a cruel, long, and thin knife with a sharp point. Close to the handle there was a sharp curve. I suspended it from the ceiling by five separate bits of thick string so that it wouldn't break.

I drove to the supermarket and brought a roll of black bin bags and thick silver tape. Not wanting to cause any damage to the house and lose my house mate his deposit, I meticulously taped them to the floor so that my blood wouldn't soak in to the grouting between the tiles.

It was strange to see so many other people shuffling around the super market like zombies. A tired young man with a packet of nappies, a group of three drunken women, all buying more alcohol. I bought aspirin to thin my blood. I greedily chewed four of them in the car on the drive back.

My plan was simple, violent, and I was convinced it would work. I would take as much aspirin as I could over the next twenty hours. If I could get some Clexane (a drug we inject in to the stomach to prevent clots from forming in patients) from work, or warfarin (another blood thinner) I'd use that as well.

I planned on lying to one of the nurses, saying I was going to teach a medical student to give sub cutaneous injections with Clexane. One I would demonstrate with, and one for the medical student to do. I would lie and take them home for myself.

I would come home from work, leave my phone in my car, and throw the keys out of my house mates window so that if I changed my mind, I couldn't ask for help. My keys would be too far from my car for me to make it with as much blood loss as I had planned. I had left a note stuck to the outside of my door: "I'm really sorry. Don't go in. Just call the police."

I would place the tip of the knife at the medial border of my sternocleidomastoid muscle (the big thick strap muscle running next to your wind pipe) and punch it with the heel of my hand. Driving its blade deep into my neck.

This would cause the knife to enter an area known as the anterior triangle. An area crowded with delicate and important arteries, veins and nerves. The carotid sheath lay here and that was my target. It contained the internal and common carotid artery as well as the internal jugular vein.

The vagus nerve and lymph nodes also found residence in this space, but weren't important for what I wanted to do.

I planned to sever one or more of these important blood vessels. Preferably all. It would be perfect if I could puncture the carotid sheath and the vessels within it.

As I fell to my knees, the knife would pull tight on the string it was suspended from and be drawn up my neck. I had to make sure I got the knife right in the hilt.

So I had to punch it hard. That sharp curve, anchoring it in place. The blade being drawn upwards as my legs gave way, destroying more structure, widening and lengthening existing lacerations.

I knew I would experience pain, but I was willing to do that. I would lose consciousness. Slump, face down, in a gently spreading pool of my own blood.

The scar would be easy to hide if my mother wanted an open casket. A closed casket would be better. Less of a reminder of the time she had wasted on me.

Then it would finally be over.

That day I drove to work in silence. I followed the speed limit, eyes open, hands on the wheel. I thought of that car as being similar to my life.

From the outside looking in, it was fantastic. Young man, sports car, driving to his fulfilling job. But inside, I was seconds away from ending my life in a smash of metal and glass.

The day passed the same as they all had for the last few months. In a constant shift from the happy doctor for his patients to that awful monologue in my head: "I fucked up last night. I got it wrong. Just make it through today and I can have a rest."

I even thought about going home and doing it then and there, "What are they going to do? Fire me? No, I've got patients to see, I'll finish today. It's the last day anyway."

At mid-day for some reason, I went to see the rota co-ordinator. She had helped me get my job and fought for my contract to be extended.

There was somebody else in the office…but I didn't care.

I told her everything.

I kept my eyes pointed on the floor and my voice quiet and even. I raised my head and saw her, the disbelief in her face. This was the last thing she or anybody else would expect from me.

"I think I need a week off," I said.

That was the first time I had knowledge that I might. It came out of nowhere, and I don't know why I said it.

I think I wanted to use that week to get better or kill myself one or the other. I figured if people thought I wasn't coming in to work anyway they wouldn't come looking for me when I didn't show up.

But there was another idea for some reason. One which came from nowhere, maybe I could get better.

Get some help and get better. Surely what I was doing wasn't right. I was told that if I worked night shifts over New Year's Eve, I could have a week off in December.

It was the middle of October. I didn't think I could do that, and left. I walked out of that office convinced that the reason I hadn't been offered compassion was that I didn't deserve it.

That the feelings I had and the desire to end my life were an appropriate response to the fundamental flaw in my soul that led my life to not be worth a week off. That I should be able to deal with things.

The spiteful voice in my head piped up again as I walked down the narrow corridors back to the wards, "Everybody else can see that I'm just being pathetic. What's more likely? Is everybody else is wrong, or am I? There's nothing wrong with me, I just wasn't put together the right way and life isn't for me. No great loss to me or anybody else."

The co-ordinator and I have discussed this conversation since, and I am told I misunderstood. I honestly think I did. Just another way depression was twisting everything.

The logical part of my mind was in overdrive.

Why did I go and tell them that? Am I ill? No... I couldn't be. What right do I have? Weak, stupid, inadequate little man looking for excuses. You just want to lie down and play the victim. You're not ill, and you need to prove it.

I pulled out my phone. I hated this phone so much. It was a window in-to the world. It was where I viewed everybody else's perfect lives and tried to convince people I lived one too.

All the while, my bathroom was covered in bin bags and blood thinners coursed through my veins. Veins which would soon be cut wide open.

'Diagnostic criteria for depression,' I typed.

I knew I wouldn't meet any of them. I was looking through them to prove I didn't have them. But then again I already had some idea what they were. There were physical symptoms such as change in appetite, early morning waking or lack of sleep, fatigue etc…

There were also the more well-known psychological symptoms such as a lack of enjoyment, persistent low mood, lack of concentration and suicidal thoughts. These symptoms had to be present for at least two weeks.

I went to the library. Reading the symptoms of depression… I still didn't want to admit it. But there it was. In black and white. Scientifically backed and produced criteria that I met.

This couldn't be right. No, it wasn't right. The voice in my head wouldn't stop.

You're making this up to make yourself feel better. More excuses. Weakling. You don't enjoy anything because you're shit at everything. You can't concentrate because you're stupid. Don't turn your inadequacy in to an illness.

I often went to the library for the peace and quiet. The same blue padded seat. The same three walled cubicle desk. The same tree, from the same window. I opened my laptop and tethered it to my phone so that I wouldn't alert anybody on the hospital Wi-Fi.

I looked at pro suicide websites for a bit. They were shockingly easy to find. Message boards upon message boards of people thinking what I thought. I was hoping for some counter argument that I could buy in to. Somebody to explain how these diagnostic criteria were wrong or I was interpreting them incorrectly. There was the odd message telling people suicide was the wrong way to go about things.

What if they were right?

I sat there in the silent library, on the thinly padded chair, looking at the walls of the three-sided desk I studied in and wrestled with the possibility that I could be sick and not weak.

I knew depression was real. I could provide psychological and biochemical explanations for it. I had seen pictures of brain scans showing functional differences in depression patients. I had worked in a mental health hospital as a student and seen it. People laid low by their own minds. I knew people I admired with it. I had lost family members to suicide, and when I read the symptoms in medical school, and again now, it was like reading a description of myself.

But for some reason I didn't want to give up on this way of thinking. It seemed the right way to be. Everything and everyone WAS awful and I was the most awful of all of it.

I opened another browser tab on my laptop.

"Online depression screening tool."

Pages of results to choose from. I thought I had to pick a validated one. One which wouldn't get it wrong. So I took a test for depression on an NHS website.

The test was called the PHQ-9. I filled in the questions and awaited my score. I scored 27/27. Full marks! The screen told me I had severe depression.

I think I took that test hoping to be shown that there was nothing wrong with me and be allowed to carry on and kill myself. Being a medic, I knew that if a patient had told me these things, I would recommend that they get help. Maybe arrange an urgent psychiatry review, or start some medication.

Depression is not something I had ever managed before as a doctor. This was the first time I seriously entertained the thought that I could have a problem. That it could be illness, not weakness. I have always trusted scientific research and process. The cold, hard, reasoning of what had to be a validated tool telling me, objectively, that I had an illness was an unexpected and uncomfortable finding.

"But I can't be ill," I told myself, "I have no reason to be! I'm just being dramatic and weak! I'm a doctor! If I was ill, I would know it! Wouldn't I?"

I pulled on this thread. It led me back to the conclusion that if a friend, loved on or patient told me that they had these problems and this score I would tell them to see the GP at the very least.

At the hospital I worked, there was an out of hours GP service next door to A&E. I doubt anybody in that A&E department liked me very much and I can't say I blamed them. I was so tired all the time, and angry. I was thoroughly unpleasant to them. Picking holes in their management plans and referrals. Being purposefully difficult. When the A&E staff rang me, I would mentally prepare myself for a battle.

All my self-loathing would spill out of my mouth, down the phone and on to the person on the other end. I walked down to the department to find out where the out of hours GP was. A kind and very competent nurse practitioner showed me where it was. They made polite conversation with me and were lovely. Despite how I could be towards them.

I felt awful. "Stupid, nasty little man. She's a good person and kind to you. Even after you've been a twat. That's the kind of person the world needs. Not you."

She told me I looked tired, and was I unwell? I joked and told her I had an STD and she laughed.

Situation avoided. But I still had to wait for the GP to open. The out of hours GP surgery started at six. I finished work at four.

When I finished, I forced myself to wait in the library before walking back down to the GP out of hours. The same thin blue chair, the same three walls.

I read up on depression. Risk factors for suicide such as being male, family history, no religion, organised plan, previous attempts, suicide note. I met all of them. I watched TED talks from suicide survivors and sufferers of depression. They were all remarkable people. I had always thought depression was for the incapable but here in front of me was proof that I was wrong.

So wrong. I noticed that, while everybody's stories had some similarities, they were all unique. How could they not be? Everybody's mind and circumstances are unique and an illness which affects those is going to be anything but uniform in how it affects sufferers.

I got up from my chair at exactly six pm and walked my practiced route to the out of hours surgery. The waiting room was empty, painted in NHS issue browns and dull reds. High ceilings and the smell of hospital cleanliness made me feel as if I was some small animal in a trap or being experimented on. I sat on the hard plastic chair and waited for the receptionist to show up.

I had turned my badge inside out so that you could only see the back of it. I didn't want anybody to know that I was a doctor.

"Everybody in this hospital knows who I am anyway. It'll get out why I'm here and nobody will believe me. I'm just looking for an excuse for the fact that I'm a prick."

I managed to talk myself into staying somehow. Through sheer effort of will, I didn't get up and go home to the release promised to me from the sharp point I had prepared to capitalise on how eager my veins and arteries were to spill their life-giving contents. The knife wasn't going anywhere, and neither was I.

The receptionist arrived and I approached the desk sheepishly. They told me I had to call a number for triage and explain why I wanted to see the doctor.

The small asymmetrically cut strip of paper I was handed had a phone number on it and I dialled it.

I huddled myself in to a small corner against the door for the public toilet. Hoping not to be seen, in case I started crying. The phone was answered quickly.

The professional, but caring, voice on the other end of the phone the same one I used to start a consultation.

The difference in the two of us was huge. Here was me, falling apart not even forty-eight hours after a suicide attempt with another one ready to go.

On the other end of the phone, a detached and professional voice. It was almost like a conversation between my professional and personal self.

I remember internally pleading, begging, praying to whatever power would hear me that I would be taken seriously. The first crack in the walls that depression had built around me.

Still though, I tried my best not to let the notes of panic and desperation creep in to my voice as I explained my symptoms. I spoke quietly, pushing myself further in to the corner. The voice asked me if I had any suicidal thoughts. I told the voice, yes, while thinking back to the killing room I had created in my bathroom, and the notes neatly arranged on my desk, the aspirin coursing through my blood preventing my platelets from aggregating if I were to start bleeding. I didn't tell them I had already tried. After some more questions it was decided that I needed to see the doctor.

I sat in the waiting room. It was silent with posters on the wall encouraging me to be vaccinated and stop smoking.

"Good advice," I thought.

The receptionist and I were the only ones in there. I heard a phone ring down the corridor and one side of a conversation I couldn't make out. I assumed it was the person I had spoken to earlier, warning the doctor they were going to have to have me admitted.

That I wasn't safe to be a doctor and that I was crazy. I stood up and began walking to the door. I could say I was feeling better and that I'd had some sleep and it was all fine now.

If they took being a doctor away from me, what was I worth to anyone?

There was nobody there to stop me and that blade potent in its lethality still hung in my bathroom.

With another great effort of will, I turned around and forced myself to sit in the chair. If this didn't help, I could go home and do it anyway. If they admitted me, I would lie to them, pretend I was better and kill myself when I got out. Thirty seconds after sitting down, the doctor called me in.

It was a young doctor. I have no hesitation in saying that they saved my life.

I walked in and tried to put on a "Sorry to bother you with this, I know it's stupid" face and posture. I tried to describe my symptoms in the kind of language you would read in a text book. "I am suffering from increasingly intrusive and persistent suicidal ideation," and "I've had anhedonia (an inability to feel joy) for about eight months."

"I'm suffering from insomnia. I haven't slept for three days now."

The doctor sat in the chair and listened to my symptoms, free of judgment. He was empathetic and personable, and made me feel cared about, and that my symptoms were genuine. It seemed strange. I had built this interaction up in my head. Created a scenario where I would be cross examined, deemed unfit to cope with life. Told I couldn't be a doctor.

Instead, I was treated like a person in pain who needed help.

When I look back on it now, I realise that's exactly what I was.

The decision was made to start me on medication, and I was not allowed home on my own.

I would be staying with friends. He gave me some medication and took my phone number.

If I wasn't with friends when he phoned me, he'd phone the police. I didn't tell him I'd tried to kill myself or about the room I had prepared at home.

I don't remember his name or really any specific details about the consultation.

But if he ever reads this, I want him to know he saved my life and set in motion the wheels which would lead to it becoming better than I ever thought.

I sat in my car looking at the prescription I had been given. A small amount of diazepam and Sertraline, a selective serotonin reuptake inhibitor (SSRI). It works by increasing the levels of serotonin in the brain. Serotonin is a neurotransmitter which plays a role in feeling happiness. By selectively stopped the re-uptake of serotonin by neurons the levels of serotonin in the brain increase and the symptoms of depression reduce.

I'm sure that's an oversimplification. If you want to know about all the different neurological pathways involved in happiness and how the medications we use for depression work on them, there are much better doctors than me to tell you or even better books to read.

We don't really understand the brain that well, despite all the advances, and a lot of the medications we use to treat mental health conditions are a lot like using a sledgehammer to crack a walnut.

There haven't been any new anti-depressants or psychiatric drugs as a whole for quite some time. We sometimes achieve our aim but in a messy way. There must be a better way… we just haven't found it yet.

I'm going to pull aside here to talk about using medication. I have read books, blog posts, tweets and watched videos and interviews by phenomenally brave and strong people in similar situations to me and some have been against medication for their own reasons.

As a doctor, I find this view unhelpful. I was against medication until I walked out of that doctor's office.

When ill, I was of the opinion that, "It might not be a mind that works, but at least it's MY mind."

In my ill state, I thought that anti-depressants were for weak people who just couldn't cope with life.

I will attest here and now unreservedly admit that I was wrong.

Now is not the place to go in-to the pros and cons of various anti-depressants. I'm not an authority on the subject and as I said there are other doctors, nurses, books and research that do a far better job than I can do.

But I will categorically state that when I was depressed that was not 'my mind'.

It is not how or who I am. While I was recovering, I slowly realised that, but not before. Medications are not without risk or side effects and should be discussed with your doctor. They might not be the answer for you. They might not be a permanent solution for you. They are one of the tools available to us to treat mental health conditions and when used appropriately they save lives.

They saved mine.

I arrived at my friend's house and they had made me dinner. There was a teary phone call to my mother, hiding in my friend's bathroom. I felt awful for worrying her, but I just wanted my mother. I don't care if that sounds like something a child would say. Sometimes we just want to be cared for and comforted.

I heard the sadness in her voice. The audible longing she had to simply look after me. Her asking me to just come home. Telling me she'd stop what she was doing and come and get me. Two hours wasn't a long drive, she said. I imagined how she would have been after me killing myself, reading my suicide note, planning my funeral, sorting my things.

If my funeral would be like my family members and what would she be like there. How would she react on my birthday and at Christmas… I didn't know what to think any more.

I was starting to think she might not feel relief, it might destroy her. She wanted to speak to my friend on the phone to make sure I was safe. He asked what her name was, and I told him Samantha.

"Hi, is this Samantha?" He asked on the phone. Samantha isn't my mother's name. Everyone laughed.

That night I thought I'd try and drink my problems away. I've never done that before, but I'd done a lot of things I've never done before that day.

Chapter Six
Rock Bottom

The next morning, I woke up on my friend's sofa, still in yesterday's clothes. I smacked my lips, my tongue and mouth glued together by thick spittle. Lifting my head rewarded me with an intense throbbing and a sudden desire to vomit.

I thought back to the night before, the diazepam, the wine and the whiskey all came flooding back to me. I could still taste them on my breath. I belched and was reminded again of them: "Evil, fat disgusting pig."

Water was a necessary evil, and nursed with small sips over the next thirty minutes. Then, as the hangover sunk its teeth in, I tried to go over what had actually happened yesterday.

I regretted coming here.

I played over the day before in my head back to the smallest detail. The corridors I took and the people I waved at on the way. How self-conscious I felt in the waiting room. Thought back to the feeling of when I let my self-erected defences crumble, and the pleading notes enter my voice as I was on the phone booking my appointment.

The colour of the door frame I had huddled against, when making the call. And how I fully expected the voice triaging me on the end of the phone to tell me there was no need for me to be seen and that it wasn't a medical matter.

Becoming vulnerable and being turned away would have been a real blow, and pushed me deeper down this hole I was in.

That prescription had been so heavy in my jacket.

I had been afraid to touch it, kept my hands out of the pocket I had stuffed it in to. I had watched the doctor type in to the computer as we spoke. Knowing that once they had coded me as depressed it was on my records forever. Digitally applying that label. My all-too human feelings reduced to zeros and ones in a computer.

I understood how patients could see doctors as detached sometimes. Having an air of superiority about them.

We type, as you detail the unravelling of your mind: The most significant and awful experiences of your life being responded to with one of the most pedestrian tasks available.

After the consultation, I remembered choosing not to wear my coat on the cold walk to my car so that I could do at least one thing that day that was an act of strength. It was a small victory. A victory for what… I have no idea.

Driving to my friend's house. Turning up, teary-eyed and broken on their door. Putting them out. Of course they had taken me in. They were good people. Now they were lumbered with a man in his thirties, hungover on their sofa after spending the night alternating between making jokes and welling up with tears, drinking their booze and taking diazepam.

"How could you be so weak and selfish, Perry?! How could you let yourself be such an imposition?! They probably just wanted to go to bed and you ruined their night."

I left the house. In the back of the taxi, I vomited on the seats. After paying for the cleaning, I shuffled back into my house and got into bed.

Thoughts about how these kind, well-adjusted people had to put up with me simply would not stop. I was dragging them down with me. They hadn't done anything to make me think that, but the nicer they had been to me, the guiltier I felt.

I knew that ten feet away there was a way out of all of this. The cold, silver metal of the knife was perfectly still at the end of the rope it was tied to, and I lay in bed just looking at it for a while. It was tempting. More than tempting. It almost seemed like an obligation. I would pace the room. The war between life and death fought in my own head. The option of suicide wasn't going anywhere I decided. I didn't want to die feeling like this and looking like this.

So I went to bed. I didn't sleep, I just tried to come to terms with the fact that I had set myself on this path of being a patient.

They say doctors make the worst patients. In our minds we are separate from our patients. Not better or having authority over, but separate from illness in some way. We were stood up talking to them in a position of being the fixer or the healer. That badge of office around our neck occasionally wielded to listen to their chest and confirm or deny our suspicions. They were lying in their bed or sat in their chair. Frightened, and sometimes, embarrassed. Tubes in and out of them… in the role of the patient.

To adopt the role of the patient for a mental health condition was utterly alien to me and I couldn't do it. I knew I couldn't do it and I was glad that the knife was there.

The room was cold and dark and my bed was my sanctuary. I lay there as still and silent as I could and, perversely, for a while my pounding head protected me from the tyranny of my own mind.

Once I had braved water and painkillers, the consequences of last night began to recede and were replaced by an internal monologue of pure spite. All of the thoughts I had been having all day turned up to eleven.

"It's right in there. Some feet away from me. An end to this and I can't keep putting people out life I have been. Do yourself and everyone else a favour and go and meet death."

After three or four hours of this, when the hangover had completely gone, (and I had forced down a coffee) I decided I had to do at least one useful thing. Something useful so that I could have a small amount of dignity left after the last twenty-four hours.

The memory of my reflection in my friend's bathroom mirror as I was on the phone to my mother just kept coming into my mind all day. Such a small, weak, wretched creature, feeling sorry for itself and expecting help. It was as if a conveyer belt led me to the bathroom.

I taped a pillow case over the bathroom mirror so that I wouldn't have to look at myself and gripped the knife. I had always imagined doing it facing the door, but after some thought I decided it didn't matter much, but I'd do it facing away, anyway.

The knife was there, just as still as it had always been.

I was jealous of its stillness and its purpose.

I gripped the plastic handle with my left hand, plucking it from the air and placed the spiteful tip just to the right of my wind pipe.

After a day of the dull pains, of regret and embarrassment…the sharp, precise pain of it was refreshing and I took a moment to savour it.

Some small part of me was shrieking. Demanding to know what I was doing. I had done so many things I had said I would never do.

That I didn't need to do because I thought was strong. Too strong to need help. I had seen a doctor, turned up on my friend's door, throwing myself at them and expecting kindness and help.

Things I would have expected a patient or a friend to do, but was embarrassed to do myself, and here I was undoing it all.

If I killed myself all that would be for nothing. But I had already failed to kill myself. It was mass production that had kept me alive, not a change of heart or divine intervention.

I should be dead already. What did this matter?

I lifted my right hand and prepared to strike the handle of the knife driving it in to my neck. Three dimensional models I had used to learn anatomy showing red arteries, blue veins and yellow nerves. All skin and muscle removed rotating on a black background pressed at me, creating a pressure in my temples. And there I stood.

Some useless idiot with a knife at his own neck and his hand ready to strike it. Ready to die hungover in his underpants. I wanted to die. I needed to die, and other people needed it too.

But there was a small chance that I was wrong. That I was ill. I had been diagnosed and I should try the treatment. The two thoughts clashed around in my head.

Eventually, after remembering my mother on the phone, "Just come home," and all those people at my cousins' funeral, I let go of the knife.

I went about the rest of my day as well as I could. I think for some reason I even uploaded a video of myself playing guitar to Instagram. To do something I enjoyed and something normal. God, I made my skin crawl.

I went about the rest of my day interacted with friends and let a few of them down, which I added to my long list of regrets. But felt I had made a very clear decision about things now. I was going to fight.

I resolved that this was in fact rock bottom. And, that as usual take that had the answers. The only way was indeed "up". Sleep was my priority and I self-medicated with diazepam, anti-histamines and some other drugs I had foolishly purchased from the internet. It wasn't a refreshing sleep or even a restful sleep. I woke up feeling worse.

Exhausted, and at a loss. But it had been some degree of stillness, maybe even peace, and that was enough in some ways. It's amazing what a night's sleep can do for you. You'd be amazed how often I ask a patient how they're feeling and the first thing out of their mouth is: "Terrible doctor, I hardly slept."

Even if they have some awful, incurable disease. It appears that sleep is king. So while my task seemed daunting, and I knew I'd fail, I thought there was a tiny chance that I wouldn't.

That I could recover something of a life. To experience happiness in some form or another, at least once more in my life.

And if I couldn't be happy, I could at least be useful.

It wasn't as simple as flipping a switch, I wrestled with myself for an hour before getting out of bed. The voice in my head telling me there was no point in shaving, no point in getting dressed and no point in going for a walk.

This was a blip. My natural state was misery and forever would be. Today was a delusion and I would be back where I belonged soon enough. Motivation was for idiots. Discipline is what I needed, "And there's no discipline here."

But I made myself do it. It was hard.

I left the knife up.

I stepped out into the cold fresh morning sunlight and walked to the chemist. I had headphones on, but no music playing so that nobody would talk to me. I looked at the people in the street, a lot of them smiling, with their families or the ubiquitous middle-aged man in lycra.

These people had meaning, purpose and things they enjoyed. I hated them for it. Each and every one of them had what I wanted.

What made them better than me? Why couldn't I have that? Because I was weak and useless! That's why. Because while everybody else made the most of their lives I wallowed in self-pity.

I wondered what I looked like, to them. Was I obviously mad? Or was I just another man? Did they even give me a second thought? Were some of them fighting their own wars in their own heads? How many of them had a knife hung from their ceiling, or wanted one there?

I kept my head down and walked. I thought over the implications of starting medication. I had always been so against it. I had thought depression was an inability to cope with our comfortable lives and that anti-depressants were a cop out. That instead of improving yourself, you reduce to the basic minimum that other people met every day.

The very characteristics of a person which drove a rich, spoiled westerner to be depressed are the ones that drove them to medications as an answer.

Three times I stopped in the street and wanted to go back home. But the sadness in my mother's voice when I spoke to her last night kept on coming back to me. If there was a one percent chance this would help. I'd take it. So I walked into the chemist and gave them my prescription.

Two weeks of the drug sertraline.

The out of hours GP hadn't given me more so that I'd have to engage with my actual GP to get more.

The inside of the pharmacy was silent. Not in the way that there was an absence of noise. But the presence of silence, one which seemed oppressive and let you hear the blood rushing in your ears. And it was so hot. My thick black coat hid what I was sure were buckets of sweat pouring from under my arms and down my back.

I felt that the woman behind the counter was judging me as I handed over that potent prescription.

"Another weakling!"

"What's he got to be depressed about?"

The internal monologue I imagined she was having was really just an extension of my own.

I picked up my medication after an agonising and very sweaty ten-minute wait. I spent those outside walking a small circuit between the pharmacy and the shop with my headphones on. I wasn't proud of myself, I didn't see it for what it was.

It is a big step in admitting that you have a problem and overcoming the poisonous thought patterns which have been default with for so long.

I walked home despising every person that I saw.

I sat on my bed and opened the paper bag. I looked at the box and slipped out the white plastic strip. I didn't know why pharmacists had to make their bags out of such loud paper.

I pushed a tablet out of the thin silver film with sertraline 50mg written over and over on it. It mirrored my thoughts exactly.

"Sertraline 50mg, Sertraline 50mg, you can't cope so you need drugs. You need Sertraline 50mg."

I was loaded with all of my own prejudices, what pharmacology of the drug I understood and even memories of me prescribing it for patients. All I could think of was that once I took this tablet, I was on anti-depressants. I was one of 'those people.'

I put it down and paced my room, pulling my hair, and digging my finger nails into it. Fuck it. I'm not taking it. I'll deal with this myself like a man should. But I had done so much! I had come so far! What would one tablet hurt? Nothing but my ego. I wanted to cry. But couldn't. Just to break down sobbing and have an outlet for all of this but it wouldn't come.

I took the sertraline and a diazepam, lay down on my bed and thanks to the remnants of the cocktail of sedatives I had taken the night before, I went to sleep.

That is how I spent that day. I don't remember too much of it really. I looked up new work out routines planning to get in the best shape of my life. Thinking that doing so would prove everybody wrong about me.

The first three hours after waking up weren't so bad, the diazepam took the edge off and I watched an explosion filled movie with impossibly good-looking people doing impossible things to save the world, get the girl, make a quip and have some kind of obligatory shirtless scene.

The diazepam wore off and I was back where I started, with the added knowledge of being a weakling on anti-depressants.

I tried to ring the GP to get an appointment. I was told to turn up at eight am tomorrow and wait to be seen. So after another sleepless night, that's what I did.

The GP was fantastic. Kind and caring. They spoke to me and interacted with me in a way that made me feel like my concerns were valid. That it wasn't just all in my head and I wasn't being dramatic.

They asked me questions that I knew were to assess my suicide risk. I lied. I knew what to say to make them less concerned. I knew to talk about future plans and support networks and express regret. Thankfully, they gave me a repeat prescription for my sertraline and quite a high dose (higher than I would normally prescribe for the hypnotically naïve, as I was) of a sleeping pill.

Sleeplessness was my main problem. I think I mentioned it at least five times in the ten-minute consultation. While I waited for that prescription from a different pharmacy, which silence had deemed unfit to visit today, I thought, "This is a high dose, but I think she's worried I'll kill myself if I don't sleep, so she's not left it to chance. Smart."

I also had a two-week sick note. I rang work to tell them. Another part of the day I knew had happened but I don't remember that conversation at all.

That night I took the tablet and I slept: For ten glorious hours. I woke up in the morning.

I dreaded looking at my phone after waking up. The numbers in the top right corner normally said something like 01:12 or 03:16.

They may as well have been saying, "Fuck you."

This morning they said 09:25.

I actually smiled.

I felt better. Just knowing I could sleep was such a relief. If I could sleep, that was some kind of escape from under the shadow that had been chasing me.

So now, I just had to figure out how to fill two weeks off.

Chapter Seven
Two Weeks Off

The prospect of two weeks off work was both terrifying and a relief.

I was terrified of what it meant. My depression had gotten the best of me and I needed time off due to this illness. Not a 'real' illness, like dysentery or small pox, but one I viewed as a symptom of my own weakness.

I was angry at myself on multiple levels.

Firstly, for needing to take the time off. But now, As I tentatively took the first steps into admitting that I had a problem… I was becoming angry at myself for letting it get so bad.

"How could I have been so stupid?"

I'll admit I was frightened. My thoughts were the enemy here, the thing which had led me to the end of that belt to having a knife hanging from my ceiling.

Now, without the distraction of work, it was just me and them. The medication I had started takes a few weeks to have an effect so my mood probably wouldn't increase very quickly. It would be a slow thing, one day I might notice I don't feel quite as bad.

At least that's what I had been told.

But now I had a new mental path to tread. One which would lead me away from paying so much attention to my thoughts. The thoughts I had been unable to realise were harming me. As somebody who had always prided himself on his intellect and ability to notice things, this stung.

The fact is that being a doctor is emotionally, physically and intellectually demanding. It puts strain on your social life and relationships and the culture of personal and professional excellence endemic within makes these things worse.

There is a phenomenon known as 'burn out', it was coined in the 1970's. Burn out is physical and psychological exhaustion related to chronic stressful situations, most often used in relation to jobs.

In a wonderful British medical journal article about the history of burnout it was shown that air traffic controllers with better psychological health were deemed more resilient (some had even seen military service) more often went on to develop burn out.

They cited poor training environments, constantly changing shift patterns and a lack of support amongst the key causative factors. Any doctors or nurses reading this will empathise with this, I am sure. Others may as well.

It seemed that the greater the demands a person placed on themselves the more likely they were to experience burn out. (1)

The first day off was difficult.

My housemate was a locum as well, so he was at home with me. I spent most of the day in my room.

The zopiclone from the night before was lingering over me, and preventing me from doing much. I don't really remember much, apart from getting a text from some of the other doctors in my team asking if I was ok.

One of whom was my junior and I thought it was my job to look after them. But here they were checking up on me. I felt this as another blow to my pride.

I wanted to be productive, to improve myself. I was going to go to the gym and train hard. Study for some exams and play some guitar. I thought this could be a good thing for me and an opportunity to show strength rather than weakness. To have something to show for, this time off.

I was placing more demands on myself. The time off was meant to be spent recovering and resting. But I still couldn't see that. Instead, I was just fuelling the fire. I was putting more demands on myself already.

Instead of viewing their messages as showing concern for my wellbeing that same oppressive shadow that coloured my perspective on everything turned it and twisted it in to something ugly.

I was convinced they were getting information on my 'illness' so that they could use it to stop me being a doctor. I was convinced that I wasn't fit for it, and was a danger to patients.

This is a common reason why doctors do not seek for help for their illness. But I doubt that it is limited to them. Mental health problems, unfortunately, still have a stigma attached to them. Sufferers, with their already distorted and harsh self-view cannot fathom that their families or colleagues or team mates would view their condition with sympathy and understanding. I know that I couldn't.

Instead, I was convinced that I would be thrown to the wolves: stripped of my license and cut off from the medical profession. Of course this was only proper.

Could a 'mad' doctor be a safe one?

The next day I managed a shower and a shave to leave the house. There was a beautiful park, a five minutes' walk away. I walked around it in silence. On the walk there was a long straight path with tall beautiful trees creating a cathedral-like vaulted ceiling. The colours of autumn were pierced by an uncharacteristically blue sky as they converged from either side. It felt protective. It helped to calm me. The cool breeze brushed my face. At times I would close my eyes and concentrate on the feeling of it, on the sounds from the leaves and the dogs barking.

I was lucky to be alive.

There was no last-minute change of heart in my story. No deep and meaningful reason for me being alive. The belt I used was cheap, and the hole I cut created a weak point. That's all there was.

But here I was. Alive.

As I stood there, eyes closed under that golden ceiling, the cool breeze washing over me and I genuinely appreciated it.

I was lucky to be here, doing this, simply standing in a park was a privilege for me I had no real right to.

I stood there for five or ten minutes mulling this thought over. Eyes closed. I must've looked odd to the people walking by me. But there I was. This soothing, almost calm feeling passed, but as I walked, I tried to come back to it.

It was the first pleasant thing my mind had done in years. I alternated between this and my head racing with thoughts of being struck off. I messaged my team asking if the consultants had said anything about me. I was a locum. Why would they keep a mad locum on the team? They could get someone better than me. But as I sat there by a river, returning to my thoughts of appreciation for being alive. Watching a heron on a rock survey the currents for whichever fish was unfortunate enough to pass his way... I found myself a little less hopeless and a little more peaceful.

One of the most insidious and vindictive ways in which depression affected me was robbing me of my concentration and enjoyment. As I have said before, I had always had hobbies. Playing the guitar, reading, wargaming, movies and anything sci-fi. Like most 'nerdy' people, I enjoy giving my attention to things on a deep level. Most people have something they enjoy the minutia of.

Football fans will know hundreds of dates and scores and transfer values. Fans of the Kardashians will probably know facts and stories about them. It's a big part of finding enjoyment in things: paying attention, enjoying the subtleties of things.

When you're depressed, you can't do that. You don't see the point in learning some stupid fucking song. In painting another nerdy model. You're never going to play for anyone, your models are for kids. Even the things you can't enjoy but have to do, filling in forms, shopping, your mind isn't there.

You can't concentrate for longer than a few minutes. You can't retain what your fingers need to do to play the song or what that sentence was you just read. And like that, it traps you. Unable to escape with anything resembling joy, interest or application of thought, you are left subjected to your thoughts.

Since your thoughts are part of the problem, you become trapped in a spiral. Every attempt to get out of it is proving you can't do anything and nothing matters. It pulls you deeper down.

With nothing to distract me, I was left with the frustration of not being able to do all of these things I had decided I would.

My housemate was very kind, and bought me the new Spiderman game for the PlayStation. This provided me hours of distraction. It quieted my mind. It was still hard to concentrate on and I wasn't very good at it. But this helped. It made me think less. I was more present in the moment and not in my own head.

This seemingly benign and juvenile observation I acquired while swinging through New York set me on what I consider to be the most useful pattern of thought I have ever had in my entire life.

It went like this.

My problem was partly in my mind. My thought patterns were negative but I had proved through two different methods (playing PlayStation and going for a walk) that they didn't have to be constant. So then there must be a way of altering the way I thought, so that I could be free from them.

I had already done this with so many things. Everyone has. Where most people would see a swollen leg and their reflex thought would be, "Oooooh, they need to see a doctor."

I would think about whether it was an infection, a blood clot, or the failure of a different organ like the heart liver or kidneys to blame.

So I could change my thought pattern. Everybody could. I just needed to find the best way to do it. I looked into CBT and even had some sessions, but it wasn't really for me.

But the real eureka moment came when I downloaded an app.

The first three minutes of mindfulness meditation spent sat in the sofa trying to concentrate on my breath were, to be blunt, agonising.

I resented even three minutes away from trying to improve myself (Despite being so low functioning that I had done nothing of the sort. Only made myself more ill).

But I persisted. I sat there focusing on the feeling of my breath coming in and out of my body. Every time my mind wandered, I brought it back to my breath.

Sometimes quicker than others, and it was difficult. It was amazing how noisy my mind was, even when I was supposedly at rest. Mostly, it was an uncomfortable experience that left me more anxious than when I started.

"What kind of idiot can't concentrate for three minutes?"

But I had read that mindfulness was helpful for people in my situation so I decided to do some research. A quick internet search showed me innumerable articles of various degrees of trustworthiness ranging from the anecdotal blog post to the blinded clinical trial.

I read through the benefits it had on depression, sleeping, attention span and anxiety and decided this was worth my time. I had a lot of time now. A further three times that day I sat down for three minutes. Focused on my breathing, following the instructions on my app, and a further three times I hated it.

The next two weeks consisted mainly of waking up, feeling groggy from the sleeping pills, and lying in bed.

My mind flitted between: "Get up and make the most of the day!" and "What's the point, you're useless, just stop taking your meds and kill yourself, will you?"

I forced myself to take the sertraline and every day it got a little bit easier. My mood still hadn't really changed, but I took the knife down.

Peeled the bin bags off the floor and stuffed them in to the bin. I received supportive texts from friends and family which actually penetrated the misery and made me feel cared for.

I played the PlayStation, and got into the swing of it (Marvel, I await your law suit). All in all, I had some kind of routine.

I still barely ate and for me to not eat was unheard of. But I would force myself to eat fruit and sometimes was even hungry. I was feeling slightly better and the meditation was becoming easier.

After a few days I was up to five-minute sessions and sometimes I would even enjoy them.

Then, one day out of nowhere, I noticed my heart was racing – no, not racing, that doesn't do it justice. It felt as if it was going to beat out of my chest. Even that seems like an overly tired metaphor, but it really is what it felt like.

My favourite movie is "Alien" and it felt like one of the titular characters was about to explode out of me. I thought I had VT from the medication (a dangerous, very fast heart rhythm, one of the ones that defibrillators work on). I put my hand on my wrist and checked my pulse.

Over 150 bpm easily. It felt like the bottom had fallen out of my stomach. Nausea pounced on me so suddenly it took me aback, and I had to make a conscious effort not to vomit where I stood.

It was as if somebody had poured a bucket of ice water over my head and it never stopped coming. My palms where sweating, my breathing quickened and I thought I was going to die.

The doctors had both warned me about the side effects of sertraline and one of them being anxiety. It is utterly incomprehensible to someone who's never had to endure it. But the phrase anxiety attack is not a misnomer.

I felt under attack. No warning. No relenting, and nothing I could do. Just a full-frontal assault on my slowly cultivated, fragile peace: by a bombardment of what I can only describe as a feeling of panic, terror and dread all in once.

I can remember exactly where I was when this happened. I was walking from my lounge to my kitchen and just passing through the door. I can tell you what was on the table, what was in my hands.

It is imprinted so clearly in my mind that I wonder if I will ever be able to forget it.

When I was in year ten, I had a fight on the back of a school bus. The other boy was taller than me and bigger than me. Something had gone on with someone stealing my brother's hat. I won the fight, and he was left with black eyes and a bloody nose (He's a lot bigger than me now and he should know that I'm very sorry).

The police came to my house and I wasn't fazed... Until it turned out he was in year eight, I was fifteen and he was twelve. The next day, I was called to the headmaster's office to find out if I would be expelled.

That feeling you will have experienced when awaiting a bollocking or being caught in the middle of something you shouldn't be caught doing. The way your heart races, your skin goes clammy and your insides turn to ice.

That's as close I can get to describing this. But that feeling is still only a taste of what was happening to me. It was like comparing a sensible family car going as fast as it can to a drag racer. Different leagues. It would be more intense or less intense at times, but never completely leaving for two whole weeks.

When I worked in A&E, due to our frustration and the services being stretched to breaking point by under staffing and low morale, along with the poor treatment of staff, as well as an ageing population, it put untold pressures on the service.

Coupled with misuse of services, poor lifestyle choices leading to chronic diseases which must be managed but could be prevented by better living, we would often see presentations such as 'panic attack' and roll our eyes a bit.

It's not because we don't care, but in A&E we often deal with people who will die within the next few minutes if you don't do something. So our perspective is a little off.

I can honestly say I thought I was going to die. It felt as if I was going to die. I cannot blame people who don't know what's going on for going to A&E with an anxiety attack.

I would. I nearly did!

I let this thought roll around in my head and came to the conclusion that I was going to let this make me a better doctor.

Everyone has their own perspective and it's valid. I resolved to try and use this to be more understanding, empathetic and more patient.

These anxiety attacks even began to appear on my daily walk around the park. I spent an absolutely awful half an hour, as quickly as I could, trying to work off the adrenaline that must be coursing through my body. I was propelled by every thunderous heartbeat that thundered in my ears. I walked as fast as I could. Did pull ups on the outdoor gym. Dug my nails in to my palms, and eventually it passed.

I kept working on my meditation. I viewed it (and still do) as a skill, one that must be learned and continuously improved.

The only way to improve a skill is through practice. So I practiced. After a week I could manage a ten-minute session and began to look forward to it. It was the first thing I did in the day and the last thing at night.

Now, when these thoughts (which I'm sure you can imagine what they are by now, I don't need to drive home the point) cropped up in my head, I simply did not engage in them.

I just let them pass. I say it was simple because it is.

But it's not easy. Sometimes I would find that I had been ruminating or having suicidal thoughts for ten or fifteen minutes without even realising it.

I would want to get cross with myself, tell myself I wasn't supposed to be doing this anymore. And sometimes I did. But sometimes I wouldn't. Sometimes I would just let it go, let the thought pass without chasing it and I could tell I was better off for it.

Rarely when I was meditating, I would experience a pleasant tingling sensation. Sometimes, between my eyebrows and sometimes along the backs of my forearms. I quite enjoyed that, and it became a bit of an incentive to keep up the habit. As good as it was for my thoughts, I have to say I didn't find it all helpful for the anxiety.

After about ten days off I felt well enough to drive.

The anxiety attacks were a lot less frequent and I was becoming used to them. I hadn't found a way around them, but they were passing, so I decided to give it time. I decided to make the one-hundred-and-twenty-mile drive back to Coventry to see my mother.

She had phoned me every day and messaged me in between. Not in a smothering way, but it was obvious she was concerned. I don't really remember much about the trip. Just the broad strokes of it. But I do remember sitting on the sofa for hours talking to her. She listened to me so patiently and there was so much love in her face when she looked at me. I stared at that face. I imprinted every single part of it on my memory. Paid attention to every word said, treating the sound of her voice like something precious. Making sure I would never forget it.

We had nearly lost her to cancer a few years before, just as she had lost her own mother, and I don't know what I would have done without her.

My feelings of appreciation which had been first noticed in that park under that golden ceiling magnified a hundred-fold. I hated myself that I wasn't more like her. She had survived cancer, a broken marriage, her own mother and grandparents dying all while having three children that she did an excellent job of raising.

She never moaned or complained once. People might say it strange for a thirty-year-old man to want to be like his mother. But I do. And those people can fuck off.

As I write this, she doesn't know about me trying to hang myself. I'd imagine I'll have to tell her before she reads this. But it's better than hating myself for doing something which could hurt somebody I love so much and who loves me.

I see it as a marker of just how very ill I was.

During the last few days of my time off, I noticed that I was feeling much better. Not acutely. It wasn't like scratching an itch or pulling a thorn out, but one day I noticed I just didn't feel so hopeless.

I concentrated on a book and I laughed a few times. I was eating and getting some more sleep without the zopiclone.

Spurred on by my success with the meditation and trying to cultivate a feeling of appreciation, I looked in to other non-pharmacological methods of managing my depression.

I have tried it all and gave it all a decent period of time. Things I never thought I would try but I never thought I'd be meditating three times a day and that had helped. I tried it all. Gratitude journaling, Yoga, I figured my brisk one hour walks every day counted as enough exercise for now.

I looked into different forms of meditation but mindfulness was really working for me and I enjoyed it so I decided to stick with that.

I would watch more TED talks and interviews with famous people who had depression. Read blogs and BMJ articles about burn out and depression amongst doctors. All of this served to show me that there was something wrong. There was an illness and I was suffering from it. It wasn't because I was weak. I genuinely think I had a genetic predisposition to it (there is a known genetic link).

A lot of risk factors for suicide (family history, a high-pressure job, being male, young, just started medication and access to means to carry it out) and those two things coupled with my job and my own dysfunctional mindset all combined to create the conditions for what I now think of as a break down.

But depression can strike anybody.

Chester Bennington of Linkin Park whose songs I grew up with. Winston Churchill, who has been voted the greatest Briton ever. Even Robin Williams. whom until the news of his death, was only associated with joy.

I wasn't myself again just yet. But I knew I didn't want to be another suicide. In hindsight, I probably should have had more time away from work, but I felt I needed to go back.

Armed with my new tool kit earned through mindful meditation. alongside a bit of chemical correction from my medication and a realisation that I had in fact been ill, I was going back.

Chapter Eight
Back to Work

I really felt I had come a long way in the two weeks off. Despite this, I didn't sleep the night before I went back to work. I lay awake worrying about what people would say. Would I remember how to be a doctor? What If I couldn't put in a cannula or a catheter? What if I missed a diagnosis or an allergy? What if everybody knew why I had been off and decided I couldn't make decisions anymore?

While staring at the ceiling, I imagined people there to greet me at the door. They would be polite but hold me firmly by the back of the arm and lead me in to an office.

Here I would be sat down and in polite managerial speak (in line with trust policy of course) they would tell me I would no longer be working there, before leading me by the arm off the site. They would probably place their hands on top of my head as I got in to my car, the same way the police did with criminals.

Of course, I tried my new mindfulness techniques but none of it helped. It was inescapable. It was one thing to get better and manage your mind when you're on your own, in your nice quiet house, sleeping as you like, able to do as you like. Where external stressors were at a minimum while being surrounded by understanding people.

But it would be another thing to be in a hospital, dealing with the same thoughts which had laid me low and without any of the safety nets I'd had at home. On top of that, the demands which had led me to neglect myself would return and I didn't know if I was strong enough to deal with them.

But I had to go back to work. Two weeks off was plenty for most illnesses.

Some people who had surgery were back sooner than that. Of course I could go back.

I got up and got dressed. Deliberated over the choice of shirt (which one says, "No, I haven't got depression and I definitely haven't tried to hang myself?")

I brushed my teeth without wanting to punch the man in the mirror, which was a definite improvement. I took my happy pill with a black coffee and set off to work.

My hands were on the steering wheel and following the speed limit the whole way.

There was nobody at the door waiting for me.

No chat in the office, and I walked onto the ward to see the face of the F1 on the team sat at the computer getting the list of patients we had to see ready for the day as they always did. They were very good like that.

They said they were glad to have me back and I could tell they meant it. She knew what had been going on and wed been in contact while I was off and were so kind and supportive.

One of my registrars had also been aware, he and his wife had been particularly fantastic having me over for dinner and listening to me talk. I really appreciated that.

The ward round proceeded without incident. That wonderful British characteristic of acting like nothing had happened and carrying on won out over my own self-consciousness and any curiosity from my colleagues.

We got on with the ward round. Me smiling at the patients while writing in the notes. Trying to make the odd joke to try and break some of that thick palpable tension and prove to everyone else and myself that I was back too and OK.

"Glad to have you back," said one of my consultants, "What was wrong with you?"

"It's personal," I replied.

"Oh." they said. Their voice contained that high pitched quality that only those denied an answer to what they felt to be a reasonable question could muster.

Their eyebrows were raised so much they threatened to leave their face entirely. Well... what was I meant to say?

"Actually, I had something of a suicidal breakdown, I tried to hang myself but failed because of the low-quality materials in whatever sweatshop churned out the belt I used. Then I spent two weeks convinced I was going to die and sedating myself. But anyway... here I am! Please trust me with your patients!"

I would have been too embarrassed to tell them the real reason I had been off.

I hate to say it, but I don't think I was alone in thinking that mental illness and particularly depression is a sign of weakness. The environments of doctors and other professionals are rife with this idea. But it is in no way limited to them. The idea of it has been around for so long and permeated so deep into our collective consciousness that the sufferer can't help but view it as such.

The hero overcomes their struggles no matter what.

Books, movies and legends have all taught us this and everyone, particularly doctors, want to be a hero. At least a little bit.

This makes talking about it so much harder. It also makes it harder to seek help. You're not the hero in this story and that can be hard to admit to yourself whether you're a doctor or not. Worse still, there's no external agent you can blame it on. No corporeal villain in this story. You're putting yourself through this without knowing how or why.

As a doctor, it's hard to reach out and admit that we have mental health problem.

Especially when we're used to diagnosing illness in terms of aberrant biochemical processes, trauma and infective organisms. You can't identify depression on an X-ray.

There's no blood test for it. It's all 'feelings' and 'words' and I think that a lot of people fall into this trap.

There are some known biochemical causes for low mood. People suffering with an underactive thyroid can suffer with a low mood and fatigue.

These are physical problems we can understand. They have psychological symptoms but more often than not, if you correct the physical imbalance the mood improves.

Some of the qualities which make a good doctor, nurse or physio such as altruism, holding yourself to a high standard and a desire to see things improved, are exactly what make us more likely to suffer from depression.

In a sinking, bloated, bureaucratic behemoth like the NHS trying to change things for the better while battling understaffing and over use, increasing patient expectations and the demands of an ageing population, something has to give.

Unfortunately for me, and many others, it was my mind.

But we keep working. The stakes can be so high, yet how can we not? What could be a more important job than making sure the woman in the bed you're looking after who is someone's wife and grandmother is well?

The other problem is that sadness, stress and anxiety are, like it or not, part of life. They are a huge part of anybody's life and an even bigger part of a doctor's.

We not only have our own problems to deal with, but spend our days surrounded by other peoples, playing our part in it. Sometimes, despite our best efforts, there is no good outcome, and the sadness is all there is.

It would be foolish to pretend otherwise. There are times when sagging under the weight of sadness is appropriate. This is almost invariably when some kind of tragedy has befallen somebody. The death of a loved one is awful. Imagine being surrounded by people losing loved ones. The loss of a job is awful, but not as bad as having one so bad that people throw up with nerves before a shift. But what about when you're just sad and numb without a reason? It's not your loved one who's just died.

You earn OK money, don't you? You need to just get a grip, don't you? It could be worse. There are people worse off than you. What about those poor people with cancer? Well… yes there were people with cancer. And I was jealous of them. A little bit less now, but my two weeks off hadn't been a miracle. I still envied them. I just knew that I shouldn't.

Whenever I walked in to a new room with somebody in it that I hadn't seen since my return, my face burned. I'm sure it must have been visible from the other side of the ward. It was the kind of burning you could feel in your cheeks and the tops of your ears. The kind that can only be generated by extreme self-consciousness backed up by the knowledge that people would be talking about you.

I kept my head down and just did my work. In every conversation I had with people I was overly professional and as short as I could make it.

Not because I wasn't pleased to see them or to be there, but because I just didn't want to show any weakness.

Looking back, it seems ridiculous that I was still pre occupied with weakness, but I was. I obviously still had a long way to go. I wanted so much not to be noticed.

I was convinced every conversation between nurses was about me. Every laugh was at my expense. I imagined them whispering to each other pointing at me. Observing me. Looking for the tell-tale signs of the mentally unwell. Looking up to see if everyone was staring at me became a habit, and if they weren't staring at me, I'd assume that they just had been, and I had caught them moments after they turned their head away.

That day, a few people who I worked with the most and knew me best said they were glad to have me back and asked how I felt.

"Better, thanks." was my stock response. It was delivered flat and monotone. I was just so pre occupied with not letting any weakness show I forgot to show any warmth or appreciation for the concern I was receiving.

I had asked my F1 to tell everybody that I'd had to have time off for treatment for an STD. Typical me. Turning everything in to a joke. But I think it was obvious why I had been off.

The few weeks before when I hadn't been sleeping several people had asked how I was and they were genuinely concerned. They told me that I needed a rest and some time off but at the time I couldn't think of anything worse.

I was quiet, I didn't talk to anybody, and spent any time I wasn't working in the library, where it was almost silent and mostly still. Not doing anything.

Just sitting there with the lie of studying for exams fed to people so as not to arouse suspicion. The fear of being 'found out' ever present.

A few people, either less sensitive, or less aware, would ask, "What's up with you?" in an accusatory tone and I would tell them I was recovering from an STD.

They rolled their eyes and walked away, probably muttering something about me being an idiot. But at least it stopped questions. I would hide in toilets or treatment rooms and try and pull myself together gripping the worktops, squeezing them like some kind of stress-ball. A hard, unyielding, sterile, and clinical stress-ball. The kind of thing that would have had no give in it until it broke completely.

I could relate.

Doctors have been known to eat lunch in a variety of ways. Some of the most popular being the over-priced sandwich on the walk back from the shop where you bought it to the ward, in the mess or one of the most popular choices…not at all. In this hospital, we mostly ate lunch in the mess. The mess is like a common room for doctors and between one and two we would all sit and eat lunch.

On my first day back, it was the scene of what I hope was the most covert panic attack in human history. There were just too many people, and too much noise.

A few people had asked me why I was so quiet but nothing special. No clear precipitant. Nobody said, "You can't have been that depressed if you didn't actually manage to kill yourself. Why did you even have time off?" to me.

(Except myself.) But, again, the bucket of ice and the pounding heart appeared.

I felt as if I was sweating through my shirt and had to leave. Power-walking isn't a sport I've ever really considered. But the performance I put on to get to the other end of the hospital that day was probably worthy of it.

I didn't eat with other people for a while after that.

That day, and many others, were simply about getting through the day. I still did my job and I did it well. I know the consultants were aware of the situation. It would have been unfair and unsafe not to tell them and they were keeping an eye on me.

Nobody mentioned any problems to me. I was a locum. They didn't have to keep me on, and I offered to resign so that they could have somebody better.

"Nobody wants a mad doctor."

But they told me not to be silly and that wasn't necessary. But I was quiet, and a few nurses told me they thought they'd annoyed me because I would walk around with a miserable face and not talk to anybody.

That was very unlike me, and I was known for things like noticing the cleaner's new haircut and telling them it looked nice, and making people laugh.

Now, I was staring at the floor and not talking, hiding in the library to eat my lunch and having panic attacks at work.

But my mood was stable.

I still had suicidal thoughts, but no intention to carry them out. When they would arrive in my mind, unbidden and without warning, I tried to remember not to engage with them. To simply let them pass: "Like a cloud across a clear blue sky," as the friendly voice in the app had told me.

But it was hard. Hard to focus on that deep breath I was taking, and not the fact that despite all your hard work and the medication and the time off, all I could think about was that in that cupboard there was enough morphine to stop myself breathing in a pleasant enough way.

No pain. No nothing. Just peace.

I kept up my medication and my meditation and over the next week or two I came out of my shell a bit.

The days became less difficult and the anxiety all but disappeared. I had a few honest and frank conversations with people who knew why I had been off and they all responded with sympathy and understanding.

"It's good that you can talk about it," was a common theme. I used to hear people talk about mental health and raising awareness and respond unkindly. I'm embarrassed to say that now.

I used to think that we live in the information age. Not a day goes by that I'm not exposed to some kind of mental health problem. In the news, on the television or scrolling through my social media feeds. I was perfectly aware! A lot of these people need to just "man up" I would think.

"Inability to deal with their cushy lives."

I knew that there were genuine mental illnesses. I'd worked in a psychiatric hospital. I'd seen it. But psychosis and mania were obvious. They were the presence of something. The presence of delusions and hallucinations. Of disordered thoughts and wild clothes and hair.

Depression was largely an absence. An absence of happiness, of sleep, of hope, and of kindness toward yourself. Of any feeling at all really.

I thought depression for the most part was just people not appreciating what they had. At least that's what I used to think. I was so wrong. So very wrong. I regret thinking the way I did. And if nothing else, this entire experience has made me a more compassionate and understanding person and doctor.

My new found appreciation of being alive had me questioning just what I wanted to do with my second chance.

I'm not really one for the whole act of God thing or the here for a reason thing, and if you are, that's great. If it works for you, then even better.

But I knew I couldn't waste this. I knew that I had to have a shift in my priorities from what I thought I could achieve and acquire to what I enjoyed and could appreciate.

I kept thinking back to being under the arches of those trees by my house. Feeling the breeze on my face. I needed more of that. Less of the other stuff.

The endless cycle of upgrading and progressing in medicine and many other careers just wasn't sustainable for me anymore. The surgical lifestyle of staying late, night shifts, twenty-four hours on call as a registrar and being called out of bed at two am when you're a consultant in his mid-forties didn't seem like the best idea for somebody with depression.

I sat with some colleagues who filled the same senior house officer gaps in the rota as me. Some in training, some locums. Several of them, not all of them, lamented the amount of time they had spent in work, the stress they felt because of it and how it followed them home. The Derision from their bosses and the opportunities missed because of obligations to their career.

Every single one could recall an incidence where they had done extra work or stayed late only to be told that their work wasn't good enough (without the offer of helpful or constructive criticism) or to manage their time better and they wouldn't have to stay late.

Was this really what I wanted?

I thought long and hard about how I wanted to live my life and what made me happy. Having gone so long without feeling happiness, and having worked so hard to try and get some back, I decided to make a change.

To consider avenues I never had before. I had been doing the same thing my whole life, and it hadn't worked. That tired, old definition of insanity we've all heard wasn't going to apply to me now that I was determined not to be mad any more.

In surgery, the job was interesting and challenging, the cases and the patients and the colleagues were fantastic.

But I had to face facts.

To live that high pressured, work centric life. It wasn't sustainable for me. I had to have a rethink.

This was a very uncomfortable thing for me to realise. The whole reason I had gone to medical school had been to become a surgeon. And here I was, barely three weeks after a suicide attempt, considering turning my back on it?

Was I over reacting? Was this a knee jerk reaction? Only time would tell. But in my head, the whole thing came down to this: which mistake would I rather make?

Spend more time in work when I shouldn't have? Or not spend as much time in work when I could have?

When I thought of it like that, it actually became pretty simple.

I've seen a lot of people die.

And not one of them said that they wish they'd worked more on their death bed.

After speaking to colleagues, my own research, and many, many lists comparing pros with cons of various specialities, I was considering options I never would have before. One that included leaving medicine entirely.

Though, despite how hard it was and how much it had taken out of me, I knew it was what I wanted to do.

I just needed something else in my life. I needed to have time for my, family and friends. My hobbies, and to rest and relax. Sustaining a reasonable sleep pattern was incredibly important to my mind, so that was a priority.

So, I decided to become a GP. I initially saw myself as a failure for 'throwing in the towel' and making that decision. I have heard people in similar positions to me say that they have 'given up' and are going to become a GP.

For some reason, hospital doctors (including me) considered GP to be the soft option.

If you're not sure about what it is, you can just 'Send it in' to A&E.

That they weren't good enough to be surgeons, or didn't have the work ethic to handle the hospital life style.

GPs are able to manage dozens of patients in a day without blood tests and X-rays, ready within an hour.

Without a senior you can ask for advice at any time.

All of this was within a ten-minute consultation window. In this culture of 'follow your dreams' and, also, 'be the hardest worker in the room!' settling for anything other than the most gruelling path can almost seem like a cop out.

But I had let go of that idea. I just wanted to be a good doctor, do my best for patients, and keep getting myself better.

You're no good to anybody sick. And that's not just doctors. It seems to me that GPs deserve just as much respect as any doctor and that this pathological mindset of venerating work ethic in medicine is responsible for a good deal of the demise of morale seen in the NHS.

The better work-life balance should give me more time to simply enjoy life. I was enjoying being a doctor again now, and I planned to continue doing so.

That feeling was coming back, and I felt privileged to be helping patients.

I didn't mind working hard, but I just couldn't let it rule my life.

I had worked nights most of my working life and been fine. It had even been a source of pride: "Oh, Perry's so hard working, he's been on nights you know."

But now I had to put my pride aside, and do what was best for me so that I could do the best for my patients. I would have time to play music again, read again. Basically, I had a second chance at life now, and I wasn't going to lose it to work.

I didn't view this as weakness or as giving up. More that I accepted the reality of the situation, and was honest and frank with myself about my priorities. This took a considerable amount of mental wrangling on my part, and even now I still have my doubts.

I read in the news about some new surgical technology or wonder drug and itch to be a part of it.

To contribute something significant to the world.

But I know I can do that by just applying myself to whatever I do and by being kind… which is something we can all do.

I don't think you need to be a doctor to appreciate that working less might make your life more enjoyable.

I immediately stopped doing night shifts at the hospital. I offered to resign again, so that they could fill my post with somebody who would work night shifts. Again, the hospital was kind and told me they wanted me to keep working there.

I told them why I couldn't work at night. That it put me back on the path I had been on. But they still asked me to, a few times.

I don't think this is due to them being thoughtless, just the pressures that they were under and the enormous amount of rota gaps. I stopped picking up extra shifts and stopped thinking of projects and studying for exams. It was a revelation!

I had always thought that you never turned down work and that you should always be striving to better yourself. But this shift to just enjoying things and appreciating them was amazing.

Now that I was no longer putting so much pressure on myself to work, I was enjoying everything else more. It was something I made a conscious effort to carry over to every part of my life.

In the gym, I didn't set myself goals anymore such as bench press double your bodyweight, or run a five-minute mile. Instead I just went and did what I fancied.

When I was playing guitar, I wasn't thinking, "You'll never be in a band, what's the point?"

I just played songs and things I enjoyed.

And you know what? I'm fitter than I've been in a long time, and enjoying music again.

I was still having trouble sleeping, but in no way reliant on sleeping tablets and my mood could be low at times, but now I was definitely on the mend.

Some days were a little bit easier than others. My self-loathing and tendency to think negatively were especially prevalent in social interactions.

Thankfully, it was becoming easier to spot when this was happening and I could take a deep breath, focus on it and let the thoughts pass.

Now armed with my hard-won insight, I could recognise this and it has since become a habit.

People who knew I had been depressed where the hardest to be around. Not through a fault of their own, but through what I thought they were thinking.

Some days that silver packet I kept by my toothbrush was the easiest thing in the world to open, and take a pill from. Other days it was one of the hardest. But I carried on.

The medication repaired my biochemical imbalances and the anxiety was negligible.

In the month before my suicide attempt, and the two weeks after, I had lost about a stone through a mixture of having no appetite or interest in food and anxiety induced vomiting.

But one night, getting home after a day of all the things which used to fill me with dread and an enthusiasm for suicide, my evening gym session was followed by an alarmingly large bowl of cheesy pasta followed by an even more alarmingly large belch.

I sat back on my sofa, appreciating the food I had just eaten and for some reason, this was a watershed moment for me.

The light at the end of the tunnel was a lot brighter now.

Chapter Nine
B

There was a colleague of mine called 'B' who worked with me at the same time as my illness nearly got the better of me. I didn't really know them very well, and we definitely weren't close. I had spoken to them before a few times. Often, as we all sat in the mess drinking coffee, or eating lunch, we would have banter with each other, but no more than I did with anybody else.

They had been exposed to the non-stop barrage of crude jokes that acted as my suit of armour and handled it well.

I was working when B started in surgery on their own, first day as a freshly pressed doctor. I liked to try and help the new doctors, trouble shooting and offering advice when I could.

Because of this, I knew the juniors well, and spoke to them quite a bit. B had approached me a few times and was doing as well as any other F1. No outward cause for concern, they seemed happy enough and were safe and competent. All in all B appeared to be doing well.

I had heard rumblings about B along the hospital rumour mill. The same way I imagined people had heard rumblings about me (This was one of the times my ability to not engage with a thought failed me and I thought about this a lot.)

In hindsight, everybody was quite obviously aware of what was going on with me. I probably wasn't as good at hiding it as I thought. They had to tolerate my bad moods and occasionally less than kind comments. They were never anything but professional and kind to me. The last few weeks had really been an eye opener for me. I had gone from doctor to patient and back again.

As well as from being the subject of gossip, to the one hearing it.

I didn't like how either of them felt.

One evening, after my time off, I was back on call and working with B.

The medication was really working well now, my mindfulness techniques were becoming a habit and I was sleeping. Feeling more human than I had in a long time and passionate about being a doctor again.

Luckily, it was a quiet shift and we had time for a cup of tea. So I made two cups and we sat on the worn out chairs in the mess next to each other.

I think B was a bit concerned about speaking to me due to, "Never knowing which version of Perry you were going to get," as one of their colleagues so eloquently put it. Initially, the conversation was a strange one. The kind of overly polite, rapid fire conversation that people trying to remain pleasant and not talk about what they really wanted to talk about go through.

B knew I had been ill and I knew they knew. I imagine B also knew I knew they had been ill.

I didn't really have a plan. I didn't even really think I had the right to speak to B about their problems. But I gently probed about how they were feeling. Going through the checklist of symptoms I had read in the library what seemed like a lifetime ago on that day I managed to convince myself that I had an illness.

"I don't want you to think I've been gossiping about you, but I've heard you might be having a tough time at the minute," I said, trying to sound relaxed.

B admitted they might be, and I asked a few more questions. I heard the answers, but most of them were followed by a joke, a reason why they were temporary or some way they were being fixed.

It was like hearing myself talk.

And I was horrified by it.

B felt hopeless, devoid of joy, and was doing far too much and burning out.

B's situation wasn't exactly the same as mine. B didn't seem to have as much social support as I had. Their family was further away, and didn't seem as close.

B also lived in hospital accommodation which can be very isolating. B's problems came from a different place than mine.

It broke my heart. I tried to keep my face looking concerned and non-judgmental and just let B talk. But as I looked at this bright, funny and intelligent young doctor, they told me things they might not have told anybody else before.

Memories of how I felt trudging around the corridors of this very hospital with my own similar thoughts hanging over me were still fresh in my mind.

I remembered how awful I felt. How hopeless. I imagined B feeling the same. But only with the added pressure of being just out of medical school and without all of the support I was lucky enough to have.

To the world B seemed to be doing fine.

But they were in pain. Still able to go on ward rounds, still able to take blood and help patients.

Saving people, but completely unable to save themselves.

I was full of anger and resentment at the system which recruited people like us and mangled and chewed us up.

Angry that they had gone through this alone, and felt so hopeless.

I wanted B to see that I had gotten better and that they could too. Stop them feeling as alone as I did. Stop them feeling so sure that nobody would understand like I had. Here was my chance.

Everything I had gone through wouldn't be for nothing.

I decided that I was going to go for broke.

After a pregnant silence in our conversation, I held my cup tightly in both hands staring at it. I didn't look up.

"I've been unwell too," my voice was low, and even.

It was the first time I'd said it out loud in work. I'd acknowledged that I'd been off, and we all knew why I had been. But it was just not said.

You don't really talk about things like that. I squeezed the cup tighter. Felt the burn on my sweating palms.

I was uncomfortable and frightened of this conversation. Because I was opening up like I hadn't ever before. Even to my counsellor. What if it didn't work? What if I couldn't help? What if they told everybody I was mad and couldn't be a doctor?

"I know," said B, sadness and compassion in their voice. I slowly put my cup down and looked up. Grateful that B had been kind to me, had understood. I remembered how alone I'd felt. How I could be sat in a room with friends or walking through town outwardly fine, but inwardly feeling so separate from all of these people.

Just wishing somebody knew what it was like, just so that I wouldn't have to be alone with it. So that they could tell me it was OK to feel like this. That it wasn't my fault and that it was OK to get help.

That's what I wanted to do for B.

I told B everything. More than I had told anybody. Even the doctors. They didn't know I'd tried to hang myself. They didn't know that my first thoughts after failing were that I was a failure. They didn't know the minutia of the struggles of day-to-day life. The guilt I live with. How catching sight of your own reflection in a car window could make you want to smash it, grab the shards of glass and drive them in to your neck. The deep longing for any feeling at all, even if it was pain or fear.

Anything that wasn't sadness or anger.

It was cathartic and I don't know how long I talked for.

I looked up to see B staring at me. I knew just from their face that they'd been feeling the same… like they were just passing through the world. They were interacting with other people but separate from them.

Their own brain was preventing them from enjoying the human experience or feeling part of it. Now that I was feeling a bit better, I knew these thoughts and feelings had been caused by my disease.

At first, as I was telling B about the way I had lived my life so for long, they were silent. As the conversation went on longer, they would interject.

They told me that that's exactly how they felt: or how they had done or thought something similar.

B became more animated, and eventually opened up more to me. B was not well.

It wasn't an entirely pessimistic conversation. Far from it. I was mindful that was how it might come across.

So I made sure to emphasise that I was feeling better now. I was realistic too. I had tried meditation that was great for me, but hard work. I had tried counselling, and that wasn't as good for me.

Different things might work for them. I didn't know. I knew it was hard to get better and it's hard to stay well too. But I also knew we didn't have to feel like this forever. Life wasn't something I had to tolerate until I died anymore.

I could see the potential to enjoy things and have some peace. The change was all because I had admitted I needed help and looked for it.

If B did, they could feel better, too.

There was a shift from me reciting my own misery to a discussion about B's own. B mentioned feeling relieved to have somebody who actually knew what it was like to talk to about it. Better yet, they could tell I was on the mend.

But it just seemed so impossible to them. So far off. And what if they weren't built for it? What if they were like this forever? I knew I'd had all these thoughts myself and it hard been a hard and uncomfortable process to overcome them. But I had done it, and planned to continue doing so.

I'd like to think I had given B some kind of hope. After our conversation I picked up my (now cold) cup and B's. I washed them and we went back to work.

We didn't mention our conversation. We carried on as if nothing happened. At the end of the shift, we exchanged phone numbers. I gave the same line which had been given to me so many times: "Call me if you need anything."

When people found out that I was depressed a lot of them asked me why I didn't talk to them.

Some of them even sounded shocked that I hadn't. Almost offended. The reason I didn't talk to anybody was that I didn't think they would understand. Even people who had been low after a tragedy... couldn't understand. Sure, they knew what it was like to be low. Everybody does. But they didn't know what it was like to be low for no reason and hate yourself for it.

I didn't want people to think I was mad, I didn't want people to think I was weak and I didn't want anybody to stop me being a doctor.

I think that unless you've been depressed it can be nearly impossible to understand. A sympathetic talk over a cup of tea is a panacea for life's woes. A break-up, or your dog dying, your kids misbehaving or falling out with a friend.

But the complete collapse of your mind and world view, might be a bit beyond the best cup of tea's healing abilities. Talking is always a good start. It was the first step on my long road to recovery. It was great to have people there for me.

But they weren't going through it. For me, talking to someone who was enduring the same was a complete revelation, it really helped.

Over the next few days B and I would chat at work, stealing the odd, "How are you feeling?"

We'd occasionally message, sometimes even going to the gym together. I even forgot that they felt the way they did sometimes. B was good at hiding their problems from themselves and everybody else.

I wondered if I was as good. If anybody else was just as good. How many people were living, feeling one way and acting another?

There were several things B said about it being OK as long as they could work and train, and it seemed so pathological to me.

That was how I had felt for all those years. But now I could tell this as not a healthy way to think. As I've said before, B's problems were similar to mine in some ways and different in lots of others.

They promised me that they would go to the doctors. Speak to their consultants. Start the ball rolling but there was always some excuse. I offered to go with them, speak to people on their behalf, help them write a letter.

Whatever would help. But nothing happened. I was never angry or frustrated. Just worried. I understood how hard it was to ask for help, but I was terrified that we were getting closer to having to rely on another belt snapping to stop something awful happening.

Then one day, after some concerning messages, I took matters out of B's hands.

I'm not a psychiatrist.

As I write this, I've had no more psychiatric training than I received in medical school and I've forgotten most of that. I want to make it clear that I wasn't trying to help B as a doctor.

I had no intention of trying to treat their problems or even diagnose them. That wasn't my place. I was trying to persuade them to get help. Point them to the professional who could help them.

I managed to make an agreement. If I came in and covered the on call for a few hours, they would see the out of hours GP like I had, and go back to work after. If that isn't an example of how presentism is, rearing its ugly head in the medical profession I don't know what is.

I drove in from home to pick up the bleep. I told everybody I was there because I was money grabbing because that's what locums do. Everybody laughed, and believed it. B was stood at the end of a long corridor and watched as I walked towards them. Out of hours, only half of the lights were on in the empty corridors.

All doors were closed, and you could have believed the hospital was deserted. B must have felt awful. They stood there, arms crossed trying their best to look nonchalant, checking their jobs list or their phone.

But I can only imagine what went through their head. I got a small wave when I was seen.

B's hand creeping up from crossed arms and making the smallest movements possible, with the kind smile on their face that you'd give somebody you want to be polite to but don't want to talk to.

"Hello," I said and flashed a big smile. "Are you ready?"

"I don't see why I have to do this," B moaned with a role of the eyes as if I was over reacting.

I put my hand out for the bleep. B protested, saying that the on call needed to be sorted. I reassured them it would be there waiting for them after they had been to the doctors and

I would leave them lots of jobs to do. I didn't think the GP would let them go back to work and I had no intention of letting them either.

Knowing how hard it was for me, and the state I was in, after my visit to the GP there was no way B was coming back to work that night.

I don't really want to go into the details about what happened that night. That is not my story to tell.

B and I still talked quite frequently for a while. They were doing well, but I think recovery was a bit harder for them. I am extremely lucky that I had fantastic social support and I don't think B did.

A colleague and I had birthdays within a few days of each other. So we decided to have a joint birthday night out. The theme was Dwayne "The Rock" Johnson in what is perhaps the greatest photographic portrait of all time.

In it, he stands proudly, like a lion or a God. A black turtle neck tucked in to blue jeans, a thick gold chain and a bum bag. I had carefully selected the most ludicrous gold chain I could find. An Aztec-printed bum bag and a turtle neck. I put it all on and walked from my house in to town excited for a night of 90's wrestling superstar themed fun.

I walked down the steps into the bar we had arranged to meet in. A good turnout. A good turnout of traitors! Behind the backs of their friends, they had conspired to dress like normal, ordinary people! Leaving me and the other birthday boy as the only two in fancy dress in a busy bar.

Well played… well played.

At some point later in the night B walked into the bar (normal clothes) and their face lit up when they saw me and they thanked me. Really thanked me.

They couldn't believe how much better they were feeling. They felt like a new person. They were back to living life rather than just existing. All the things that had seemed so far away and impossible to attain that we had talked about on that on call shift (in normal clothes) were seeming like a real possibility now! The smile on B's face was genuine and there was excitement in their voice.

The surprise hugging was something I welcomed, despite not being much of a hugger. (However, this quickly turned to regret and fear for my rib cage.)

Talking to B reminds me of how dark things were, and how far we've come. We check in on each other every now and then. I find it hard sometimes and so do they.

I know it might seem like I helped B, but B helped me too. How far B had come, and having somebody to talk to who understood things, helped me just as much as the medication.

They've come so far and I'm proud of them and anybody else who gets help.

This whole experience did a wonderful job of providing me with perspective. I had spent the last few months convinced depression was a shameful secret and I just needed to keep it to myself and get on with it.

In a strange way, I was lucky to observe the illness I had been suffering from as an outsider.

To watch somebody else go through it, while it was all so fresh in my mind. It showed me how even though at the time your thoughts make complete sense to you, they're wrong and manipulative.

How depression doesn't make you feel like you're living in a fog, but like you've had the fog lifted and you're seeing the world for what it really is.

But in that bar, with B doing their level best to give me a second waist half way up my rib cage, it dawned on me that acknowledging my illness had not only saved my own life but potentially B's as well.

Depression locks you in your own head. You think you're the only one and you can't possibly share your struggles with anybody.

Opening up to B was the right thing to do. I think I helped them. I thought back to the people who had helped me the most in the short time I had been addressing my illness. They were mostly people who had been honest and open with me about their own problems and the steps they took to fix them.

I didn't shout it from the rooftops, but I would tell the truth when I was asked about it. If I had to have a morning off for counselling, I'd say that's what I needed the morning off for.

I wasn't going to be ashamed of it or lie about it anymore.

I did this for all the other people secretly fighting their own demons.

To see that someone else was doing it out in the open might help them too.

I hope that B's story as well as my own shows people that no matter how low you get and how hopeless things seem you can get better. I hope that it proves that I'm not an isolated case.

I really hope that nobody in the position I was in, ever, has to feel as alone or desperate as I did. I hope that by writing this a few less people will.

Chapter Ten
The Human Cost of Caring

It would be easy now, to rant about how poorly my colleagues and I have been treated whilst providing anecdotes about how some people from politicians, senior management, consultants and even members of the public don't value or respect doctors, nurses, porters or pharmacists.

I could state that in 2017, 15% of NHS staff in England reported experiencing physical violence from patients.

I could tell you that in every A&E department I have ever worked in, there are posters on the wall to remind patients and their families to please not punch the nurses.

But instead, I will try to provide a picture of the general state of affairs with regards to the doctors and the toll that their job takes on their physical and mental health.

The world health organisation estimates that around 300 million people worldwide suffer with depression.

And that, at its worst, depression can lead to suicide. When compared to the general population and other professional groups doctors have the highest rate of depression with between 10 and 20% becoming depressed at some point in their careers.[1]

Suicide is the most common cause of death for men aged 20-49 in England and Wales. A frightening statistic, since suicide as a whole is now less common and its prevalence reducing in almost every group, except young men.

One doctor kills themselves every day in the US.

A Russian doctor has reported a suicide rate as high as 10% amongst his class mates.[2]

This is alarmingly high and I am not sure how much I trust this statistic. I am not for one minute suggesting the rate is similar in the UK. I am merely pointing out the global nature of the problem and its universal severity.

Around the time of the much-publicised contract imposition in England, a junior doctor tragically took their own life by walking into the sea, mentioning the health secretary by name in their suicide note.[3]

This was the only time I can think of when the toll of a doctor's work on their physical and mental health was briefly illuminated to the general public that I can remember.

Australia has declared a suicide epidemic amongst their junior doctors and now treats suicide amongst doctors as work related deaths.

Female doctors in England have up to four times the risk of suicide of the general population, and it's not just limited to doctors.

---

[1] https://www.nhs.uk/live-well/sleep-and-tiredness/why-lack-of-sleep-is-bad-for-your-health/
[2] BMJ 2017, 357:j2527
[3] BMJ 2016, 352:i1697

Nurses working in England are 23% more likely to kill themselves than the general population.

Overall, men are more likely to kill themselves. But men working in health care account for a lower proportion of suicides than the general population.

However, likely due to access to drugs, they account for the highest proportion by poisoning.

It seems reasonable to conclude that working in health care must be a contributing factor. There is a worldwide epidemic of suicide and it is disproportionately affecting doctors, nurses and other healthcare professionals. This is most likely to be multi factorial. As with most medical problems there is an interplay of genetic, physical, environmental and social factors all contributing to varying degrees.

However, there is no doubt that being hard working, having a tendency toward perfectionism and being committed to a task can all contribute to making a good doctor.

These same traits can make us take on too much, both in terms of workload and the emotional burden our work places on us. And it doesn't stop there.

We are often trying to excel in our clinical commitments as well as complete the lesser known non clinical obligations for doctors… such as exams, courses, audits, research, teaching. All this, often at the expense of our personal and family life.

The effort to do our best for our patients often seems like an uphill struggle.

In a system which seems to be designed to want us to be at our best for the paperwork, it sometimes seems the patient comes second.

We can feel like names on a spreadsheet which represents a rota, not real thinking, and feeling human beings.

It seems that every week there is an anecdote from a junior doctor who has quit due to being denied annual leave for their wedding or something similar.

You can be moved around the country as often as every six months making friendships, relationships and homes hard to maintain. Every specialty will have its own specific factors which erode the morale of doctors. In surgery you are expected to be present at all times, even after night shifts. Always present in an environment which is proven to have a higher-than-average incidence of psychopathy.

In A&E you have the drunks and the worried well, alongside the truly dark side of human nature, such as domestic violence and child abuse. All of this you are expected to cope with, alongside seven twelve hour shifts in a row and minimal breaks in work.

In geriatric medicine, discharging a patient can take months due to factors outside of your control, sometimes with the patient contracting a hospital acquired infection such as pneumonia while awaiting social care to be organised so they can return home.

All of these stressors coupled with other non-clinical factors such as fear of litigation (doctors in the UK are twice as concerned with litigation as their counterparts in France and Germany), expensive exams, college membership, General Medical council (the doctors governing body) registration, courses and insurance.

For example, if you pass all of the exams and attend all of the courses required or surgical training, pay your GMC membership, and your royal college of surgeon's membership in a single year that can cost over £4000. That's not including conferences, indemnity insurance, parking permits, stethoscopes, journals, text books and more.

Some things which seem as petty as not being able to find a parking space at work after you have paid for a permit combined with everything else, breaks us all down bit by bit.

I think I can speak for a large number of my colleagues when I say that looking after patients, operations, resuscitations and dealing with grieving families are not the most demoralising part of the job. It's hard.

Several times I have left a room after delivering bad news as quickly as I could, because of tears in my own eyes.

But you are doing what you want to do, what you are trained to do.

I can promise you that staying late for a thing like that doesn't bother most doctors one bit.

But spending two hours on the phone between GP surgeries, pharmacy and community nurses to restart a patients Warfarin when you should have already gone home without so much as a thank you can be soul crushing.

Again, it would be foolish to think this is a problem only doctors face. A full-time nurse can expect to spend nearly one fifth of their working week on paper work[4].

---

[4] https://php.nhs.uk/doctors-health-wellbeing-depression-surgeons/

It is a well-known psychological fact that chronic life stressors are more detrimental to our health than big acute events. Unfortunately, medicine exposes us to both.

But despite all this, one thing remains true amongst all health care professionals, not just doctors.

We devote enormous amounts of time and energy to our jobs, often at the detriment of our own health. We accept it because it's 'What we signed up for.'

Before they have even left school, many doctors and nurses will have chosen their A-levels accordingly. Gained excellent grades and had extra-curricular activities they hoped would make their application stand out. While doing this, they will likely have watched TV shows about doctors ranging from comedy to drama and fantasised about being a member of this profession held in such esteem by society.

I wonder if they would still have done this if they had watched a movie where doctors were four times more likely to kill themselves only to find out it was more of a documentary.

When you apply to medical school to prove that you are a well-rounded person, you must have interests and passions outside of medical school. I remember sitting in my interview telling the interviewer that I enjoyed music and the gym as well as reading. Things which I would quickly have no time for as soon as I became a doctor.

During my time at medical school, there was minimal mention of resilience training or acknowledging the stresses the job will put on you. You were correctly reminded of the privileged position you would be in. To share somebody's first or last moments of life, hear their secrets or ease their suffering is an honour afforded to few.

You were not informed that you were entering a profession that according to a Medscape survey only 60% of doctors would choose to do again.[5]

However, the minimal support I received at medical school was infinitely better than what I received when I started working.

There is little to no institutional support to help us deal with the fact that somebody we may have built a personal and important relationship with as we cared for them in their final days.

We might have thought about a patient at night, rang the ward to check up on them, or drank your coffee with because you didn't want them to be alone. They have just passed away.

Instead, you have to, "Get on with it," or follow the advice I was once given: "Have a very large glass of whiskey when you get home."

It is worth noting that a 2010 study noted that as many as 1 in 6 doctors may have substance misuse problems with alcohol being the most common panacea. The rate in the general population is 1 in 10.

There is the occasional, 'lunch time mindfulness' session advertised on various wards and in offices offered by a well-meaning member of staff, but I can think of very few doctors who have a 'lunch time.'

The British medical association has services many of which are only available in London, and there are multiple charities and local initiatives some of which I have benefited from personally. However, it seems apparent that these

---

[5] https://www.medscape.com/slideshow/uk-doctors-satisfaction-survey-6009772#17

methods are failing with around half of the young doctors thinking about leaving the country within three years of starting the job they have sacrificed large parts of their youth for.

It's not only your youth that you have to sacrifice.

Significant chunks of your free time when you finally reach the hallowed ground of being a qualified doctor are still thanklessly consumed by the necessities to deliver adequate care.

Working extra hours is something we all expect to have to do and we don't mind doing it. Covering shifts is also something we expect and we might grumble and moan about it, but we understand it needs to be done.

Due to low staffing and the occasional sickness, there can be a lot of these shifts which must be covered sometimes at short notice. So when you are asked if you can stay late because nobody else can you feel as if can't say no. In some jobs this might mean that shelves are not stacked, promotional videos not edited, or some other benign consequence.

But if there's no doctor to do the shift, then patients aren't getting their care. You could try and rope somebody else into it, but they already have enough on their plate.

Technically, I suppose the seniors could come in, but then your name would be mud. So you are trapped. You have to do it. Sometimes you will be paid for the extra work but more often it is with the promise of a shift swap which never materialises.

On top of this, certain colleagues can be simply unpleasant to you. I remember once having to tell a patient alongside my registrar that they had cancer. There was no quiet place to speak to the family and deliver this heart-breaking awful news.

There were also several urgent things happening at the same time, including an operation that needed doing that only the registrar could do. After a difficult and upsetting conversation, I was pulled aside by the ward manager and shrieked at for daring to use their office. I don't blame them.

Nurses are short with you because they're so busy and over worked and management seems devoid of humanity and out of touch with reality, and more concerned with targets than the human impact of their decisions. They are constantly tinkering, trying to solve the problems in ridiculous ways. Putting more demands on the nurses.

Implementing new IT systems with minimal training.

Instead of improving things, they often create inconvenience and frustration. In one hospital I worked in, ward managers were checking the socks of nurses to make sure they were black... perhaps it might be better to make sure your nurses were coping with their jobs?

And it's not just limited to mental health problems. Being a doctor also takes a toll on your physical health.

In 2014, senior doctors answered a survey with 44% saying that they felt being a doctor had taken a negative toll on their physical wellbeing.[6]

Doctors are less likely than others to seek help. One study had 78% of doctors saying they felt too busy looking after others to look after themselves, while an equally worryingly 55% said they would have felt ashamed to ask for help. [7]

---

[6] 3.J R Soc Med. 2017 May; 110(5): 198–207.

[7] https://php.nhs.uk/doctors-health-wellbeing-depression-surgeons/

A lack of sleep is known to be correlated with poor decision making (which doctors do a lot of) and increased risk of depression (which doctors get a lot of) yet sleep spaces on night shifts are few and far between, often curling up under hospital blankets on decades old threadbare sofas in the mess as members of other teams come and go, as bleeps go off and passersby talk loudly.

A quick look on the NHS website (the people I work for) will tell you that regular poor quality sleep is a risk factor for high blood pressure, heart disease, obesity and cancer, as well mental health problems such as depression and anxiety.[8]

Sources such as the U.S. department of defence, and business leaders have funded studies showing that executive functions and the ability to change your mind when presented with new evidence all suffer when sleep does.

The aviation industry has taken note of these findings and now has scheduled sleep breaks for pilots. Due to rota gaps, most likely caused by people not wanting to be doctors anymore, night shifts now come with a higher work load often making these sleep breaks impossible.

You are also expected to rapidly alter your sleeping patterns. You can be asked to work twelve-hour night shifts on a Friday, Saturday and Sunday and treat Monday as a day off... Even though you have worked the first 8 hours of Monday and then return to work on Tuesday morning.

For people with mental health problems such as myself, this can be particularly damaging. Of course we need to work night shifts, there have to be doctors available twenty-four

---

[8] .https://www.nhs.uk/live-well/sleep-and-tiredness/why-lack-of-sleep-is-bad-for-your-health/

hours a day. I don't think any of us expect to be able to sleep every night shift, but it might be nice if, when we could, there was somewhere other than a mouldy sofa to do it on as standard, or the effects of changing sleep cycles were recognised by rota co-ordinators.

When I was working as a locum, most people could work through a limited company (the same way a builder or plumber might) and pay lower corporation tax when you work through an agency like I did. But the government brought in legislation designed to exclude healthcare workers from this.

So I was self-employed, while missing some of the benefits of that and facing all of the drawbacks.

It's not about the money. Nobody is in healthcare for the money, I can promise you that. This is another example of how doctors and nurses are being treated. This is yet another of the one thousand cuts leading to the death of a doctor's morale.

I understand that I have painted a bleak picture of being a doctor. I hated being a doctor while I was unwell. I would tell medical students not to bother and to get out while they could. Rant at colleagues about how much I hated my job and all the things I could do instead.

There are a lot of statistics and references used to display some of the problems because I only have anecdotal experience. I can provide a more complete picture by looking at the evidence and people deserve to be informed about these things.

But what can't be expressed numerically are the benefits. From the enormous Hollywood moments where you save a life with chest compressions or administer an epi pen to the smaller, more subtle moments that almost mean more. The frightened elderly patient who smiles and holds your hand, simply because they're pleased to see you.

Or the cup of coffee and a biscuit from the nurses who take your bleep off of you for five minutes and screen your calls... Not bothering you unless it's an emergency. I am genuinely thankful for every small act of kindness like this.

I have learned my lessons the hard way. At a great personal cost. I am convinced that being a doctor is the most rewarding job I could have.

It doesn't have to be bad for our mental health. But in order for this to no longer be the case, huge changes on many levels have to be made.

Making the wellness of your staff a priority is known to improve outcomes in almost every industry other than healthcare. So why don't we do it?

Doctors encourage others to seek help all the time. so why don't we do it ourselves? Why do we have to remind people not to assault the people saving their lives?

I'm afraid I don't have the solutions to these problems but surely if we work together, we can find them.

Chapter Eleven
A New Perspective

Part of what makes healthcare professionals stay working in these stressful jobs which take such a toll on us is that we like to fix things.

In my case, preferably quite quickly.

If there was a wound then I would stitch it. If there was an infection, I would prescribe antibiotics or drain it. A patient would come in with a problem and it would be fixed. The patient would go on their way. Either home from an operation, or, if I was working in the emergency department they might be referred onto the most suitable medical speciality if appropriate, (having been on both sides of the referral conversation, I can tell you that the medical definition of the word 'appropriate' is not universal.)

Emergencies and acute problems are what drew me to medicine. Chronic diseases weren't really that interesting to me. The long-term management of heart failure never really gripped me in the same way that a patient in pulmonary oedema (a condition sometimes caused by the heart not pumping properly, where the patient's lungs fill with fluid) did.

And this mindset has led to some mistakes from me during my recovery. Setbacks and frustrations have been common, but I've done my best to persevere.

One hard thing for me is that I have a condition which I don't think can be 'cured.' There wasn't a quick solution to this particular problem.

I couldn't just perform some action and go on about my life as if it had never happened.

Instead, it has to be 'managed,

I still think of myself as depressed, even though I don't feel the same way that I did when I was diagnosed.

I think depression as a word causes some confusion.

But it's quite a simple and descriptive word.

You can depress a lever as in push it down. And that's outwardly what happens to the sufferer. They're low in mood, often slow and exhausted.

What other terminology are we supposed to use? I couldn't very well tell my brothers or friends I had anhedonia with suicidal compulsion and insomnia.

I could have used dramatic poetic language such as, "a poisonous cancer of the soul!" or, "my mind had become my enemy," but that doesn't help with standardisation and treatment.

So for now, until somebody much cleverer than I, comes up with something…we're stuck with the term 'depression.'

A lot of people will say, "Oh, I'm so depressed," when really, they're experiencing grief or just a bit sad, the same way they will say, "Oh, I'm starving," when they're really just hungry.

Or that, they have OCD, because they like to have the placemats looking neat on the table.

These are appropriate responses to life events and circumstances and it would likely be unhealthy if you didn't have them. I'm not saying that grief isn't absolutely awful and can't destroy a person. Or that grief and depression can't co-exist. What I'm trying to say – and please don't think I'm playing down people's problems is this.

The difference between somebody saying that they're starving when they've missed a meal, compared to somebody who is actually starving. (Which is a physiological state with specific features.) Is the same as somebody experiencing an appropriate grief reaction or sadness and somebody who is truly suffering with depression.

There are similarities. But under the hood they're not the same. Thanks to fMRI we are now able to see structural and functional differences in the brains of depressed patients.

Even within people diagnosed as depressed, there are different patterns seen on these scans. It we would seem that depression might have distinct physical changes associated with it. That the brains of depressed people work differently.

Some days I feel awful, almost back to how I was at my worst. There hasn't been any cause except for a lack of sleep that I can identify. But some days it just happens.

Some nights I can't sleep or I wake up at four in the morning and watch as the light around the edge of the curtains grows brighter before my alarm clock tells me it's time to get up.

Other nights I will have eight glorious hours of restful slumber and wake up feeling fantastic.

I suppose everybody just has a bad day some times. It's just that when I have a bad day, because I also have depression, I struggle to handle it.

The same way that everybody gets a cold sometimes, but somebody with chronic lung disease may be struck worse by it. So, just as they have to make changes like giving up smoking and using inhalers, I have had to make changes, like avoiding unnecessary stress and using medication.

The days can be hard. Sometimes as hard as they used to be. I can sit at home trying to think of something to do to pass the time but unable to see the point in anything. I can be out with friends and feel so separate to them, so alien that it's as if they're actors in a movie I'm watching.

Recently, at a concert, I looked around at the people enjoying themselves, couples holding each other, friends' heads tilted back, arms in the air mouths wide open screaming lyrics and couldn't help but think, "That will never be me."

But I didn't follow the thought down that rabbit hole. I just let it pass. I have tried my best to learn to manage things, and as I live with it for longer, and learn more about depression and how I handle it, I have the bad days less often.

Luckily for me, I am extremely susceptible to drugs.

During my second year in Wales, I went to Amsterdam with some friends, including my house mate and the friend who took me in after my trip to the doctors. While feeling adventurous I tried a cannabis lolly-pop. Soon after starting to eat it, I felt a pleasant fuzziness in my head and a sudden interest in my hands and all the wonderful things they could do. I rolled around on the bed telling any of my friends who would listen about the effects of this wonderful lolly-pop and how it was the best thing ever. Quickly they went to purchase more. We were in Amsterdam. You have to try it! They told the kind man in the shop about how quickly it had affected me and asked if he had any more. Like I said.

A small dose of any drug, alcohol, Oramorph or antihistamines have a profound effect on me. In this case, even the suggestion of a drug was enough as there was no cannabis in this lolly-pop at all. Just flavourings.

My lack of tolerance to any chemical is lucky for two reasons. Firstly, that it gives my friends many opportunities to tell this overrated (and not really very funny) story whenever we meet somebody new. Secondly, that I remain on a low dose of sertraline with great effect.

I won't lie, there are some side effects that are hard to deal with. Every now and then anxiety will sneak up on me, especially in big groups or when myself and people around me are drinking.

I can have quite realistic nightmares a few times a month which can be quite unpleasant. I am tired quite early in the evening and for a while my libido was greatly reduced. (Probably to just about double that of a normal man.)

But these are relatively minor. I know several people personally and professionally who have struggled to find the right medication for them.

In my case, I have found one quite quickly that works very well and with minimal side effects.

The more exotic medications used in mental health conditions can result in rapid and dramatic weight gain, sedation and other problems. I am incredibly lucky and unfortunately not everybody is. I am not an authority in any way in these medications and by doctor standards my knowledge is basic.

If you think starting them might be beneficial for you, or experiencing side effects I would strongly suggest you speak to your doctor.

So now I was taking my medication for my chronic mental health problem. I put it by my toothbrush so that I would take it every morning and kept a strip of three pills in my wallet just in case I miss a dose or wasn't at home.

But medication isn't really enough to manage most chronic conditions.

Sometimes it's not even required.

Lifestyle factors are incredibly important in conditions like diabetes and coeliac disease. The same is true for depression.

I knew that no longer pursuing a career in surgery was the right choice for me. It was a hard decision to make and one I still want to go back on sometimes.

I see friends progressing, learning more skills, operating independently and getting more responsibility. It can be painful to see. I'm pleased for them, they've all worked hard and sacrificed for it. Every single one of them deserves it.

It's just that sometimes I'd like that to be me as well. Unfortunately, the longer you have been out of medical school before beginning surgical training, the more difficult progressing is.

For example, you have to have more academic papers published to be able to become a registrar the longer the time between graduating and applying for a registrar position.

I struggle to resolve this with the two sides of myself sometimes. Moving between thinking that all that extra work is just too much stress and me wanting to be able to prove I can do anything and everything.

It's not always the obvious destructive thoughts you have to control. Sometimes it's the thoughts, which on the surface can seem positive, that lead to dark places.

The desire to try harder, to do more for other people.

These can be the ones that you have to catch, lest they lead you back down the hole you've just crawled out from.

There is no way to avoid the long hours, the night shifts and the staying late in surgery. As hard as it is for me to turn my back on the dream that made me go to medical school nearly a decade ago, I know that this is the right thing for me.

Not putting so much pressure on myself has been the single most important change I have made in my commitment to staying well. It was a hallmark of my personality. I gave up on a long-term goal of mine that I have sacrificed things I'll never get back.

It's painful, it really is. But I know that I wouldn't have been able to stay well if I would have continued.

As a locum, I could only work when hospitals have a gap in the rota. Once again, I have been incredibly lucky and almost always filled a long-term position. Meaning I had work every day.

Unfortunately this also included nights, long days and weekends. So another change I made which was a lot easier was that I would no longer work nights and keep weekends to a minimum.

This meant a drop in wages, but one of the best things that a near death experience can leave you with is a renewed sense of perspective.

I didn't value 'stuff' any more. Clothes, cars, watches. I bought all of these things, thinking they would make me happy. But as soon as that initial rush was over, the shallow pleasurable sensation that buying things gives you leaves as quickly as it comes.

All I was left with was a room full of 'stuff' that added nothing to my life.

I appreciate that my situation is an incredibly privileged one. I was earning good money and had no commitments. A lot of people with or without depression may be struggling to ends meet and some disposable income or even just not having to worry would mean the world to them. I'm not ungrateful for what I had. I'm just saying that it didn't make me truly happy.

I enjoyed driving my sports car for a bit. But then I didn't even notice. I enjoyed going out for dinner several times a week for a bit. But then it was just another meal. A shirt keeps you just as warm regardless of which logo is stitched on to the chest or whose name is in the collar. I was so much more interested in learning to appreciate things.

The old adage "You can't buy happiness" was certainly true for me. So now I work less and live more simply. I spend more time on the things I love. I improved my relationships with people and gained so much more than money can buy.

I had intermittently kept a journal, even since I was a child. I wrote a lot when I was at my lowest and I've read them back since. There was not a positive word in any of them. And definitely no gratitude. So if I spent thirty minutes every night writing down how negative my thoughts were, then it was really no wonder I never challenged them.

I indulged in my misery. Used a lot of dramatic language. The time it takes to turn a thought in to a hand-written entry creates a chance for further rumination and I would fill pages and pages with self-loathing ramblings. Suicidal thoughts and plans and even imaginary shopping lists of things I could buy to kill myself with.

This was something I could control easily. So I resolved to only write positive things down. Things I was grateful for. To me a year ago this would have been, "Useless hippy bullshit."

I would never have done it. But now I look forward to taking five minutes to just write down a few nice things that have happened to me during the day, or things I'm grateful for. Often, I'll find myself getting carried away and come up with more and more things I appreciate.

So, tell me. Is fifteen minutes scrolling through Facebook comparing your life to others before you go to sleep more productive than taking time to really think about the good things you already have?

I used to balk at stuff like this. But hey! You know what? It's working so I'll keep on doing it. I was committed to getting well and staying well so I would give this a go.

There are TED talks about gratitude and YouTube documentaries about people thanking everyone involved in their morning cup of coffee. From the Barista, to the man who built the roads that the trucks drove on to deliver the beans. It was amazing how much there was to be grateful for, when you stopped to think about it. It was also obvious that nobody could do anything alone. I felt foolish for thinking I could have gotten better on my own.

I started to make a habit of being grateful. The benefits of this are widely known and a quick Google showed me several hundred articles with photos of serene faced people sitting cross-legged by sunsets, promising me untold benefits of practising gratitude.

Some of these articles were probably a bit fantastical, guaranteeing everything from lower blood pressure and better mental health to levitation. But as an idea I was intrigued and it made sense to me. Other people must be thinking the same.

During any trip to Paperchase to find a hilarious birthday card you'll see gratitude journals for sale. In Waterstones and even Tesco you'll see books on gratitude and mindfulness. It seems like so many of us are crying out for some kind of answer to the question of what to do when you live better than Henry VIII and are still miserable.

Alongside my mindfulness, my new gratitude practice really did help to shift my thinking in a much more positive light. Even those same thoughts that plagued me months ago. Thoughts about how I didn't deserve to live in this peaceful, fair country. Having rights that people in other countries were denied. How I didn't deserve to be physically healthy. They were noticed and not engaged with. If I did engage in them, I would quickly try and turn it in to a positive.

I was grateful to live in this country, grateful for the NHS. Grateful that when my mother had cancer, top quality care wasn't an issue. Grateful that I had my health. So, here I was, less than a year from being somebody who set a timer so they wouldn't sleep too long and wouldn't read non-fiction books because they were a waste of time.

I had become a meditating practitioner of gratitude on anti-depressants.

What would people say?

I couldn't care less.

I was happier than I had been for years.

I didn't turn into some kind of non-reactive zen master overnight. (Nor do I really want to.) I just wanted more control over my thoughts. If somebody punched a wall and broke their hand, they probably should take measures not to punch a wall again. They might even have to be a bit more careful with what they do with that hand for a while.

Well, I had broken my mind by being constantly negative. And I was going to be a bit more careful with it.

It's easier to sink back in to depression than to fight it all the time.

It was a constant, low level application of effort and it was incredibly difficult. There were a lot of mistakes. A lot of times my new tool kit would slip my mind and I would ruminate on things.

I had a wonderful gift for taking something perfectly innocuous somebody had said and turning it in my head in-to some veiled insult.

That is one problem which I'm not even nearly close to solving and I really do have a long way to go. And sometimes things just get the better of me and I remember my new tool kit, but just don't bother to use it. But with time, practice and patience it's becoming easier to pull myself back once I've started.

I tried a few other things which didn't work quite so well. Yoga really isn't for me, pursuing the runners high really isn't on the cards either, and counselling I just didn't get on with. Arts and crafts were fine, computer games were better. I tried minimalism with some success.

Getting rid of half of my stuff didn't make me any happier but I wasn't sad to see it go. By half of my stuff, I mean comic books that I'd read once and put on a shelf and never looked at again. Clothes that didn't fit. Worn out shoes. Things I hadn't looked at for years.

That wasn't a transformative experience for me but hopefully some charity shops did well out of it. But it did make me re-evaluate how happy "things" made me. After much soul searching, it turned out that once you had met all your basic needs and was comfortable, the answer was: "Not very."

I now buy a lot less stuff and feel like I have more because of it.

I read philosophy which seemed largely too abstract. I really enjoyed the stoics and would recommend them to anybody who feels that they would benefit being more in control of their own thoughts. Though, I would recommend not to follow their examples too closely, since a few notable ones committed suicide. I listened to motivational speakers on podcasts and YouTube but, I always found motivation to be a bit of a trick. It arrived rapidly in a rush of endorphins and a belief that I could do anything, before leaving just as quickly as it came, leaving me feeling not much different.

If anything, I felt more of a failure because I couldn't live up to their ideals. The same with self-help books. I'm sure there are lots of things available that I could try.

Some would work and some wouldn't. Some of the things that have worked so well for me wouldn't be for everyone else.

I think everybody has their own experience of these things and no solution is universal.

But sleep. Sleep was everything to me now. As I said, I had stopped working irregular hours and changed my lifestyle so that I didn't have to work so much to afford it.

But despite all my hard work, sleep was the toughest nut to crack. I had always treated sleep as a luxury.

But it must be incredibly necessary, since we can't help but spend a third of our lives doing it.

Nearly every animal does it, so that must mean that across all that time, all those different stories of evolution and sleep has been a constant. And that must be for good reason.

I read many books on sleep, scientific papers on the benefits of sleep, listened to podcasts. Anything I could get my hands on. Sleep hygiene was a common theme. No phones for an hour before bed. Have a routine. Keep your room dark and cool. All things you've probably heard. Some of them will work for you… some won't.

Some of you will have other things you find helpful. And sometimes we just have to miss a bit of sleep, as anybody who has had children, will tell you.

But now, thanks to sticking to my routine, and really prioritising it, I enjoy nearly eight hours of sleep most nights.

It wasn't just things I had started to do as well. There were things I had to stop doing. There were a lot of behaviours and habits I had been a slave to for a very long time which I doubted were doing me or anybody else any good.

In particular: comparing myself to others.

One way I tackled this, was by applying my mindfulness and gratitude practices when I would begin to fall into this trap.

I would catch myself when I was out.

Upon seeing some incredibly handsome man, I would wish I looked like that. Or a colleague would win some prize, and I would wonder why I was so lazy and stupid.

Nowadays, I try and stop myself and be glad that in the grand scheme of things, it didn't matter how you looked, really.

Or that I should be grateful that there are people who are committed to advancing medicine and that one day me or somebody I love could benefit from it. Or better yet pleased for anybody who is doing well and is happy. Not just your friends and colleagues.

But there was one habit I had, which I felt was particularly harmful to me. That never ending thumb-controlled feed of photographs, video clips and quizzes to find out which kind of toaster you are.

Social media, to me, is a tool. It can be used for good or ill. I could have used it to keep in contact with friends, get notifications about events which might interest me or get reminded of how bad your haircut was eight years ago.

It could even be a gateway to communities of similarly minded people with similar hobbies, or interesting articles I wouldn't have found otherwise. But all I really found myself doing was comparing my own depressed mind with its constant stream of negative internal chatter to the constant stream of happiness and sanitised life I saw.

To overcompensate, I would show off on it. Guitar solos, new purchases, anything I felt would get me a "like". So many of my posts were almost me boasting about how much I was working 'sixteen hours in the library' or that 'I've worked 14 days straight.'

Much has been written about the effects of social media on mental health. Very little of it is positive, and anecdotally I can tell you it had a negative effect on mine.

Being constantly exposed to these photographs, which show perfection and these status updates which show achievements, or those wonderful never-ending friendships. It took its toll on me. During my long sleepless nights, I would scroll though my feeds. I'd see these perfect people on the other side of the glass getting married or buying their first house.

I rarely felt as alone as when I saw groups of friends I had been a part of in university, or medical school, going on holiday together or to each other's weddings. I had just broken up with my girlfriend in no small part due to my illness and at the time I loathed these people moving on with their lives so effortlessly, as mine collapsed.

If it wasn't my friends, it was some celebrity living the perfect life, with perfect teeth and hair. It doesn't take a genius to see that these cherry-picked artificial representations of human life aren't the entire story and definitely aren't attainable.

But yet we think that's how we should live. If these people can do it, why can't I?

I would see a man with a six pack and scold myself for not having one. Then eat four doughnuts. Then scold myself again. There is no way that was healthy. I refused to have my attention commoditised, especially at the expense of my mental health.

So I came off of it.

I deactivated my accounts.

I feel better for it, and I don't miss it one bit.

All of this has left me where I should have been all those years ago on the day I got into medical school, excited about practising medicine. Proud to be a doctor.

More importantly, it's made me a better doctor. I'm more patient and understanding and thanks to maintaining an altered perspective I appreciate just how much of a positive impact some of my actions make.

How much of a positive impact everybody in a hospital makes. And I love my job again!

But I leave it at the hospital door. I get home and leave work behind me. I take time to rest, to take care of myself, to do things I enjoy and to maintain these strategies which helped save my life.

Chapter Twelve
A Second Chance

I scrubbed my teeth, rinsed, spat, and looked up at the myself in the mirror. I looked better than I had done for a long time. My eyes were bright and the bags were gone.

Physically, I looked fitter than I had done for a long time. The mirror was showing me a reflection of myself.

Not an enemy, or the mobile corpse that housed my broken soul. But actually me.

A happier version of me, dare I say, a better version of me than I ever thought I could be.

I would have never thought this was possible six months ago. I had been simply enduring life before. Waiting to die. Wanting to die. Trying to die. Everything I had been through, all the pain, the hopelessness, the loss.

I still remembered it. But I had gotten through it, and the huge changes I had made in both perspective, lifestyle and values to get here had made me a better person.

I picked up my phone and read the message I had just received and spontaneously a smile spread across my face. This message made me happy and gave me something to look forward to.

I left my bathroom and read a cheap trashy novel, the kind where the authors name takes up half of the front cover in large gold letters. (For no reason other than to enjoy it.)

I didn't scold myself for not learning anything from it or it not being a classic. I just enjoyed it.

Then I sat down to meditate for twenty minutes, I noticed the thoughts that entered my head, I let them pass without reacting to them, while focusing on my breath and the feeling of being present in the world, helping me to build a space of calm within my own head.

One I could return to at any point in the day instead of going to the older, darker places I had spent years building. This was part of my routine now, and it had helped me so much. I climbed in to bed at the same time as I did every night and fell asleep quickly.

I woke up at six thirty am after sleeping straight through. I wasn't disappointed that I'd woken up any more. I didn't waste fifteen minutes of my day playing on my phone before I got out of bed like I used to.

Instead, I opened the curtains as I walked past, and looked up at the blue sky. A thought popped into my head about how this meant I could do something nice outdoors this weekend.

What a change from the kind of thoughts that used to pop in to my head. Instead of thinking about ending my life, I was planning to live it. I groggily walked to the bathroom.

That same happier person was stood on the other side of the mirror as the night before, only with much worse hair.

I brushed my teeth, my medication rattled in its plastic as I pushed one through the thin silver foil and in to my hand. I swallowed it with a glass of water.

I am grateful for the second chance at life that they had helped me have.

I was in work today, but had plans in the evening. On the way to work I genuinely laughed out loud multiple times at the podcast I was listening to.

Laughing was something I tried to do as much of as I could now. The fact that so much spontaneous joy arose in me that it burst out was still novel to me.

I had been good at faking laughter before, but this was something I had almost forgotten I could do.

I parked my car and saw a colleague in the car park. While before I would have waited in my car, pretending to be on the phone or just hoping not to be seen and walked in alone, now I got out and waved, walking in together and chatting.

I was still doing many of the same things I had done before my recovery. My day to day hadn't changed that much. But now I had more energy, I was more pleasant to be around and enjoyed being around people more. I could concentrate and I couldn't remember the last time I had even thought about harming myself. Things mattered.

I wasn't a ghost wondering through the world. My flaming mind wasn't burning away any meaning or connection to people or experiences any more. The future was no longer the space that existed so that I could suffer in it until I killed myself, it was full of possibilities for joy and connection and purpose!

Medicine was interesting to me again and patients were so much more than my job. I wanted to be here. I'd be here for free. I was just lucky they paid me.

Sure, sometimes I forgot that, and in a job this stressful I had my moments where I gave in to the desire to moan and rant. I think everybody working in a hospital does. You have to. It's like a release valve. But for the most part, I just wanted to help these people to the best of my ability.

I've not swung so far the other way that I love every second and every aspect of it. I've not changed my relentless pessimism and bleakness for sunshine and rainbows.

Paper work is still boring, being the message boy between consultants rather than them talking to each other and risk bruising their ego is still demoralising and frustrating.

Now though, I appreciate those moments when I do get to help my patients. I have learned to savour and appreciate them. I think all doctors could benefit from this. Things that might seem trivial to us can mean the world to a patient.

While reviewing a patient of mine, a patient one bed over was vomiting profusely. It just wouldn't stop. Tears were streaming down their face from the retching.

It took me less than five minutes: I spoke to the patient, put a cannula in, took some blood and prescribed some anti sickness medication.

Later that afternoon the patient was feeling much better and they were so grateful. It took less than five minutes of my time to spare that person who knows how much suffering.

I thought about how lucky I was that I got to do that. About how, if we all stopped to think about it, even the most minor things we do for patients can have a huge impact.

Later that day I got a thumbs-up from that now smiling patient, who looked pleased as punch with their cup of tea and chocolate biscuits.

Would I rather my mind focused on what I didn't have, and how my life compared to others? Or things like this? A simple question. An easy answer.

It was something we could all learn from, I think. Acts of kindness aren't limited to doctors and nurses or even the caring profession. Think how much a bunch of flowers, "Just because," or cooking someone's favourite meal could mean to them.

People would tell me how glad they were to have me back. How they had been worried about me. I didn't immediately assume they were lying.

Instead, I was honest and open. I would tell people why I had been off if they asked. Tell them there were good days and bad days. That sometimes I still struggle but was doing better. I was even making less crude jokes. Make less of a spectacle of myself.

Don't get me wrong, I was still hilarious! (But not at the expense of my dignity, anymore.)

When I moved hospitals, one of the wards got me a mug with a photo of me they'd stolen from Facebook. Another got a cake and we all had a slice. It was lovely. I couldn't help but think how lucky I was.

Later that night I went to the pub with some friends. Nothing special about it. The same thing lots of us do at the weekend. But it just meant so much to me.

I felt present, and joined in with the conversation. Laughter kept erupting from me. I wasn't drinking much, since starting medications and I wasn't drinking tonight. At one point I just looked around at how happy everybody was at the table. How the silly game we were playing had everybody cheering and booing.

The world outside of that table may as well have not existed and for a few beautiful hours I forgot all of my troubles. I didn't even notice other people in the pub or on the walk home. I definitely didn't hate them, because they were happy and I wasn't.

I just enjoyed being alive. And that is something I plan to continue doing.

My heart is pounding in my chest as I write this.

This isn't an exaggeration, I cannot believe I get to write this. To see these words in black and white, and to actually mean them, is the greatest gift I could have been given.

I was given this gift by the medical professionals who gave me their time, patience, expertise and most importantly their humanity.

By my friends and loved ones who were there when I was at my lowest, when I was foul tempered, miserable and argumentative.

By my family, who rallied around me with nothing but love and acceptance and immediately proved that all my fears about what they would think about my illness were unfounded.

I sometimes think 'gift' might be the wrong term for what I have now. I was helped, of course, but I earned this. I earned this by overcoming my misconceptions about mental health and what weakness and strength are. By taking medication. By learning new skills and trying new things, not all of which worked. By changing my priorities and perspective. By keeping going when it was difficult and looking after myself. These aren't special things that I've done. They're things that everybody can do.

I still have days where I struggle. To be honest, sometimes, I'm just so tired of fighting with myself that getting out of bed is difficult. I just want to lie down where I stand. There are days where it will take hours of rumination before I realise what I'm doing and get back to my new, helpful ways of thinking. Days where I compare myself to others. Days where I hate my job.

Some days I hate that I take medication. Some days I have hated writing this book. It's been hard to bare my soul like this. But some days, it isn't every day, and that's what it used to be. I was unsure what I wanted to do with this book once I had written it.

It was just for me at first. But seeing how I had helped B by being honest, I knew that if I could help people not feel so alone and see that recovery was possible, I had an obligation to do it.

Not as a doctor, but as a human being. And a few days ago, when I had a message telling me somebody I used to work with had killed themselves, I knew that this could be the most important thing I ever did.

Aside from being a gift from others, this is a victory for myself. A victory over the shadow in my soul. The shadow which took my drive, and my strength, and warped them into tools to beat its poisonous thoughts in to every experience of every day. In which I used my pride to try and stop me getting the help I needed.

The shadow which used my desire to help people to lead me to a suicide attempt, resolute in the belief that everybody I know and loved would thank me for removing myself from their lives.

I'm not special, I've been to school a lot more than most but I'm not special.

If I can get through this… if I can beat back that shadow, anybody can.

References

1. Brief history of burnout, BMJ 2018, 363 doi: https://doi.org/10.1136/bmj.k5268 Cite this as: BMJ 2018, 363:k5268
2. Veressayev VV. The memoirs of a physician. New York: Alfred A Knopf, 1916.
3. J R Soc Med. 2017 May, 110(5): 198–207.
4. BMJ 2016, 352:i1697
5. https://www.medscape.com/slideshow/uk-doctors-satisfaction-survey-6009772#17
6. https://www.qualitasconsortium.com/index.cfm/reference-material/fundamentals/patients-not-paperwork/
7. https://php.nhs.uk/doctors-health-wellbeing-depression-surgeons/
8. .https://www.nhs.uk/live-well/sleep-and-tiredness/why-lack-of-sleep-is-bad-for-your-health/